WILLIAM JAMES

# MODERNITY AND POLITICAL THOUGHT

Series Editor: Morton Schoolman
State University of New York at Albany

This unique collection of original studies of the great figures in the history of political and social thought critically examines their contributions to our understanding of modernity, its constitution, and the promise and problems latent within it. These works are written by some of the finest theorists of our time for scholars and students of the social sciences and humanities.

The Augustine Imperative: A Reflection on the Politics of Morality
   by *William E. Connolly*
Emerson and Self-Reliance
   by *George Kateb*
Edmund Burke: Modernity, Politics, and Aesthetics
   by *Stephen K. White*
Jean-Jacques Rosseau: The Politics of the Ordinary
   by *Tracy B. Strong*
Michel Foucault and the Politics of Freedom
   by *Thomas L. Dumm*
Reading "Adam Smith": Desire, History, and Value
   by *Michael J. Shapiro*
Thomas Hobbes: Skepticism, Individuality, and Chastened Politics
   by *Richard E. Flathman*
Thoreau's Nature: Ethics, Politics, and the Wild
   by *Jane Bennett*
G. W. F. Hagel: Modernity and Politics
   by *Fred R. Dallmayr*
The Reluctant Modernism of Hannah Arendt
   by *Seyla Benhabib*
William James: Politics in the Pluriverse
   by *Kennan Ferguson*

# WILLIAM JAMES
## Politics in the Pluriverse

Kennan Ferguson

ROWMAN & LITTLEFIELD PUBLISHERS, INC.
*Lanham • Boulder • New York • Toronto • Plymouth, UK*

ROWMAN & LITTLEFIELD PUBLISHERS, INC.

Published in the United States of America
by Rowman & Littlefield Publishers, Inc.
A wholly owned subsidiary of The Rowman & Littlefield Publishing Group, Inc.
4501 Forbes Boulevard, Suite 200, Lanham, Maryland 20706
www.rowmanlittlefield.com

Estover Road
Plymouth PL6 7PY
United Kingdom

Copyright © 2007 by Rowman & Littlefield Publishers, Inc.

*All rights reserved.* No part of this publication may be reproduced, stored in a retrieval system, or transmitted in any form or by any means, electronic, mechanical, photocopying, recording, or otherwise, without the prior permission of the publisher.

British Library Cataloguing in Publication Information Available

**Library of Congress Cataloging-in-Publication Data**

Ferguson, Kennan, 1968–
  William James : politics in the pluriverse / Kennan Ferguson.
    p. cm.
  Includes index.
  ISBN-13: 978-0-7425-2326-5 (cloth : alk. paper)
  ISBN-10: 0-7425-2326-8 (cloth : alk. paper)
  ISBN-13: 978-0-7425-2327-2 (pbk. : alk. paper)
  ISBN-10: 0-7425-2327-6 (pbk. : alk. paper)
    1. James, William, 1842–1910—Political and social views. 2. Political science—Philosophy. 3. Pluralism—Political aspects. I. Title.
JC213.J35F47 2007
320.092—dc22                                                2007004346

Printed in the United States of America

∞™ The paper used in this publication meets the minimum requirements of American National Standard for Information Sciences—Permanence of Paper for Printed Library Materials, ANSI/NISO Z39.48-1992.

# Contents

| | |
|---|---|
| Series Editor's Introduction<br>  *Morton Schoolman* | vii |
| Preface | xxi |
| Acknowledgments | xxvii |
| 1  The Universe and the Pluriverse | 1 |
| 2  The Descent of Pluralism | 15 |
| 3  Sovereignty, Self-Determination, and the Nation | 33 |
| 4  *La Philosophie Américaine*: James, Bergson, and Reverberations of Intercontinental Pluralism | 51 |
| 5  Onticology Recapitulates Philosophy | 73 |
| Conclusion | 89 |
| Bibliography | 95 |
| Index | 105 |
| About the Author | 111 |

# Series Editor's Introduction

KENNAN FERGUSON'S *William James: Politics in the Pluriverse* is the eleventh volume in Rowman & Littlefield's **Modernity and Political Thought** series and it follows publication of the new editions of the original ten volumes in the series.[1] Initially designed to include only these ten volumes, **Modernity and Political Thought** has been expanded and will include—in addition to Ferguson's work on James—forthcoming studies of Marx by Wendy Brown; Merleau-Ponty by Diana Coole; Aquinas by Shadia Drury; Thomas More by Peter Euben; *Publius* by Jason Frank; Rorty by Michael Gibbons; Freud by James Glass; Mill by Kirstie McClure; Rawls by Donald Moon; Nietzsche by David Owen; Schmitt by Kam Shapiro; William Connolly by Kathleen Skerrett; Machiavelli by Miguel Vatter; and Sheldon Wolin by Nicholas Xenos. Moreover, I expect this list to grow in the future. As those who are familiar with the previous works of these authors will expect, these studies adopt a variety of approaches and pose importantly different questions. As contributors to **Modernity and Political Thought**, their efforts also are commonly devoted to critically examining the contributions that major political theorists have made to our understanding of modernity—its constitution and the problems, promises, and dangers latent within it.

Kennan Ferguson's earlier work places him among the increasing number of political theorists who have taken what I would refer to as "the aesthetic turn" in political theory. While this is a development whose history is complex and beyond the confines of this brief introduction, it is a turn to aesthetics to illuminate theoretical problems at the center of contemporary political thought. Ferguson's study of James can be seen as a natural outgrowth of his first book, *The Politics of Judgment: Aesthetics, Identity, and Political Theory*, in which he elaborated and defended a radically pluralistic conception of aesthetic practices and the ways they constitute individual and cultural identity.[2] A review of the main lines of argument belonging to *The Politics of Judgment* (hereafter, *PJ*) will show us how its aesthetic explorations next led Ferguson to James's conception of pluralism, which is steadily making inroads into contemporary political theory and, as it does so, is fostering the development of a new theory of pluralism and pluralist politics.[3]

To be sure, it is the work of art, its qualities and its properties that first come to mind whenever questions of "aesthetics" are raised. Ferguson, however, pursues a much different direction. Aesthetics, far more generally, refers to questions of value—specifically to what cultural groups but also individuals *value*, in the broadest sense, on every occasion they value life or a way of life, or place value on anything in life or on anything and everything a way of life includes. Valuing, or judgment, then, in Ferguson's view circulates throughout everyday experience, so much so that it is arguably constitutive of ordinary experiences and is to be valued as among its most important dimensions. Indeed, can we imagine any experience to which we do not in some way and some form attach value? As valuing and the infinitely plural forms in which it appears, life is aesthetic, through and through. And since valuing entails the expression and representation, contestation, and negotiation of values, often passionate and sometimes violent (though not necessarily so), values are the media through which we construct, affirm, disavow, revise, and reconstruct who and what we are as individuals and groups. Aesthetics, in other words, concentrates our attention on valuing as the universal activity and experience constitutive of identity, rather than the other way around, as is commonly held. The aesthetics of valuing becomes, in Ferguson's estimation, the ground of politics and the soil on which politics flourishes. Bringing valuing, identity, and politics tightly together, his argument highlights a set of relationships that correspond to a theoretical *gestalt*. By virtue of its connection to the constitution of identity, to the plurality of the ways of valuing and to what is valued, politics is intrinsically aesthetic and cannot be otherwise.

Ferguson looks to Kant, Nietzsche, and Wittgenstein for the aesthetic theories around which to frame and develop this argument. Though not unproblematically, Kant's *Critique of Judgment* serves as a cornerstone of his effort, as it enables him to begin to secure the all-important aesthetic connections between valuing (judgment), identity, and politics. Of those concerns that are most important to the third *Critique*, Ferguson narrows his focus to Kant's analysis of the shortcomings of the objectivist and subjectivist theories of aesthetic judgment. At issue here is Kant's contribution to a model of aesthetic judgment that differentiated between right and wrong—rather than true and false—judgments of value on the grounds of their agreement—or lack of agreement—on a common taste that takes its measure from a universalizable consent flowing from the identity of a people.

Ferguson recalls Kant's insistence on disinterestedness and communicability as the qualities of aesthetic judgments from which a *sensus communis* can be forged—a community of subjects whose agreement to share certain values they judge to be right defines them culturally or, in a phrase, constitutes their identity. Built around the sharing of values, such a cultural identity emerges from deliberative discussion and debate about questions of judgment, which are informed ideally by dispassionate thinking and a pedagogical sensibility, that is, by a good faith willingness to teach and persuade others and to be taught and persuaded by them. Cultural identity is consequently political, while its aspiration to be inclusive of the deliberatively formed judgments of all subjects, to achieve universality, as it were, elevates its politics to the level of a higher, transcendental reason and morality. Through Kant's model of aesthetic judgment, Ferguson presents us with an image of the public sphere that integrates value, identity, and politics, while also demonstrating how collective and personal identity can be founded *on* aesthetic judgment. With Kantian aesthetics, Ferguson displaces the customary expectation that identity always precedes and is the ground for the judgments we make, the values we affirm and those we reject. Not only is the contrary often the case, but the constitution of identity through aesthetic judgment also points toward the Nietzschean ideal to which Ferguson next wants to lead us—how we can remake ourselves through our valuing, how we can become the objects of our own aesthetic activity, how collectively or personally we can become works of art.

As Ferguson recognizes, Nietzsche's aesthetics incorporates many of the aspects of Kant's aesthetic theory, which he summarizes nicely:

> For both, the aesthetic realm is the most human aspect of existence, making life possible by making it meaningful. For both, the aesthetic sense is the most vital of the senses, awakening us to the possibilities of the world. And for both, the aesthetic experience is at the heart of the very nature of commonality, of the transmission of experience. (*PJ*, 12)

Yet, it is the ways in which Nietzsche is distinguished critically from Kant that pushes Ferguson's project forward. Nietzsche's emphasis on creativity against Kant's stress on judgment now enters into the foreground, the former evincing an appreciation for the aggressive, artistic energy entering into the aesthetic activity of judging that the latter neglects in favor of a more studied orientation on the part of both the individual and collective subject. And Nietzsche's attachment to the higher value of noncommunal solitary judgment is also brought to the fore, as is his corresponding hostility toward the

Kantian allegiance to the universalizable commonality of the *sensus communis* for diminishing the value of judgments that are unique or outside those commonly agreed upon. In effect, Ferguson's move from Kant to Nietzsche is one that deepens the pluralism he wants aesthetic theory to support. Nietzsche's concept of aesthetic creativity pluralizes the value judgments that come into being as viable sources for a pluralization of the forms of being—cultures no less than individuals—that can unfold from such new valuations. For Nietzsche, the pluralism of valuing that Kant affirmed is no longer held hostage by the latter's communitarian politics and its moral constraints, but is as emancipated from politics and morality as the autonomous work of art ideally speaking. It is clear that Ferguson admires in Nietzsche an aesthetics that to a certain extent opposes the aesthetics he admires in Kant.

If Ferguson discovers in Nietzsche a chastening of the political and moral desideratum of Kant's aesthetics, he discovers in Wittgenstein what he believes would cure Nietzsche of apparent other philosophical excesses, though not without possible theoretical costs. Wittgenstein's theory of meaning first would distinguish among types of judgments relative to the cultural, linguistic context in which they are socially constructed, thus confining aesthetic judgments to those contexts culturally reserved for aesthetic matters. Judgment in general, like meaning in general, is intrinsic to language, and judgments of any particular kinds are intrinsic to the particular ways in which a language enables and constrains judgment, which, to paraphrase Ferguson, is captured by the linguistic space where we make communal sense of the world. The language we use to make one sort of judgment is inappropriate to make a judgment that requires other meanings drawn from different contexts. Rather, the way judgments *have* been made is the way judgments *ought* to be made. Immediately, the implication here is that no Nietzschean privilege could be accorded to the point of view of the artist or to aesthetic creativity as a source of new judgments. Judgments must be rendered and appreciated only within their venues of established aesthetic languages and their meanings, none of which are permitted to stray from their specialized curricular applications. Likewise, Kant's idea of a public transformation of value seems threatened, as contextually determined judgments militate against the possibility of values achieving a universal approbation that could be intelligible outside of the far narrower contexts in which they originated. So much so does Wittgenstein at first appear to build a prison of meaning, that Ferguson ponders how it would allow us ever to have any new aesthetic experiences of the world.

Wittgenstein's understanding of judgment finally sustains the connection between judgment, identity, and politics to which Ferguson lays claim as the foundations of his argument. Since making judgments appropriate to the objects judged supposes knowledge of how a language is used—which is what enables someone to know the variety of judgments a language enables—to judge is at the same time to take part in a system of culturally defined meanings, to assume a cultural identity, and to be implicated in a language that is the offspring of politically as well as culturally constituted contexts of meaning. Where, though, in Wittgenstein's aesthetics lies the element of pluralism that Ferguson so highly prizes? Although Wittgenstein's theory of language seems to be a prison that locks up meaning in compartmentalized cells that limit the sorts of judgments we can make, Ferguson assigns a "muted optimism," as he calls it, to the possibility that the constellations of meaning peculiar to each cell could nurture each other, essentially allowing the meanings each contained to be recreated in light of each other. The plurality of differentiated meanings would be expanded to include new meanings and hence new ways in which values could be formed and judgments could be made. The integrity of context would be respected, while each discrete context of meaning would become internally pluralistic, cosmopolitan so to speak, which in turn would facilitate the pluralistic creation of valuing and judgment that derives from the ways that contexts of meaning engage—inspire, teach, and learn from—one another. Finally, this internal and external pluralization of contexts of meaning fuels a third form of pluralism. Individuals and groups whose contexts of meaning undergo revision and transformation through the cross-fertilization of reciprocal engagement, have access to novel sources of valuing from which their cultural identities can be revised and transformed. In short, a theory of judgment that at the outset appeared designed to thwart an aesthetic theory of social life and its pluralistic flowerings in the end becomes its reluctant ally.

Of the many virtues of Ferguson's work on the relation between aesthetics and the constitution of identity, he brings Kant's, Nietzsche's, and Wittgenstein's aesthetic theories to life by showing how they can improve our understanding of political problems that beset modernity. As he does so, he tests each of their powers of illumination against competing theoretical approaches to the same problems.

In precisely this way, he weighs the comparative utility of the Kantian aesthetic against two rival theoretical perspectives—race-based and performative theories—by bringing all three to bear on the question of what insights they can offer into the political and cultural grounds on which a people reproduces and recreates its identity. Race-based theories of cultural identification, he reminds us, take cultural identities to be literally embodied and consequently function to convert our cultural constructions of race into naturalistic, essentialist indicators of cultural identity. The "truth" of cultural identity that such racial markers pretend to disclose provides an ideological justification for existing cultural inequalities, which essentialist representations also reproduce by suppressing insight into their political origin as the ground for their political redress. As Ferguson expresses it perfectly,

> Race is where identities . . . are made substantial and corporeal: the body becomes ideological dogma. The syndication of visibility and essence creates unshakable political entities. (*PJ*, 34)

More to the point of Ferguson's interest in the aesthetic dimensions of identity, race-based theories of culture are blind to the ways cultures create their own identities independent of racial markers, blind to how culture changes and evolves. Performative theories of cultural identity, though an improvement over raced-based theories, also fail to rise to the level of an aesthetic grasp of cultural vicissitudes. From the performative standpoint, which deconstructs race-based essentialist claims, identity is not only a contingent and mutable achievement, but is the product of the actions in which cultural groups and their members are actually and regularly engaged. Actions create culture; changes in actions can change culture. It is the very matter of what counts as a performative action, however, that Ferguson problematizes. Performative theory privileges actions that are corporeal, neglecting the significance of actions that do not meet performative criteria, such as how different people who perform similar or even the same actions differently experience their world while doing so. Identity, in other words, is created in ways not covered by performance, specifically by a people's own self-understandings, which also were invisible to race-based theories.

A Kantian approach to the aesthetics of cultural identity fastens onto that which the racial and performative theories miss. An aesthetically conceptualized identity thematizes the "centrality of judgment," which is to say the centrality of *valuing*, itself the centrally most important activity in the formation of who we are. Are we not the summations of what and whom we value? To the extent to which we are, our valuing can be said to lend coherence to our identities, a coherence that persists over time as cultural traditions and customs, as cultural memory. At the same time, are these memories of past judgments not regularly teased, tempted, and challenged by our new opportunities for valuing differently, even if only in the direction of a small valuational difference? Since they are, judgment can be said to be contingent as well as historical and liable in the course of such regular provocations to partially reconstitute the identity that previously was the settled storehouse of culturally determined valuations. It is precisely this sort of logic that, in Ferguson's judgment, seems to capture the dynamic relationship among valuing, culture, and identity, as Kant theorized it. Cultural groups form a sense—meanings, values, awarenesses, appreciations, rationalities—that its members hold in common as the source of their self-concept, their identity. And as identity's commonsense gels and dissolves and gels again in the course of the daily play of the infinite interactions through which judgments are asserted, compared, contested, withdrawn, suspended, and sustained, it thus follows a course by which ever new possibilities for different judgments offer ever new possibilities for different identities. Kant, Ferguson proposes, succeeds in formalizing these contingent processes of aesthetic judgment in a model of the public sphere charged with the work of determining the commonsense, the common values, the common culture—identity. To Ferguson's mind, this appears to be the far more important aspect of Kant's theory of aesthetic judgment than the way it endangers its creative features with the encumbrance of universality.

When Ferguson next fleshes out Nietzsche's aesthetics with reference to one of the most important world historical events in late modernity—the dissolution of the Soviet empire—this appraisal of Kant undergoes adjustment. Among the many implications of the collapse of the Soviet Union, Ferguson explains, its impact on American cultural life is among the most salient, for it effectively exploded the ideological nucleus—the polarity of communism and anti-communism—around which American cultural identity for decades had been formed.

As a set of cultural self-understandings, as a "global subjectivity" situated among all other global subjects, American cultural identity rests upon the ways Americans understand the world, in large part constructed through the ways the world is "mapped." Mapping, conventionally referring to the representation of geographical space, in this context refers to the representation of *cultural space*, specifically to how cultures discursively represent each other— a practice that positions cultures in relation to one another and structures the perceptions and interactions determinative of their futures and fates. For decades American cultural identity—its moral integrity, democratic legitimacy, military and economic will to power, self-confidence, self-esteem, and self-reliance—was constructed through the mapping of the Soviet Union as the "other" of America, a map largely the work of political discourse generated by the American state, in the broad sense. Such an identity becomes precarious without its "other" to maintain its self-certainty, so the disappearance of Soviet communism "endanger[s] U.S. subjectivity," in Ferguson's words, a development that requires that there be invented "alternative oppositions to shore up the threatened [American] moral distinctiveness." (*PJ*, 55) How Nietzsche would mount an attack on the Kantian aspects uncovered by Ferguson's analysis of this dynamic can readily be seen. All those components of American cultural identity whose definition and certainty are secured in the construction of Soviet "otherness" amount to none other than a Kantian *sensus communis*—a moral sense, a sense of democratic legitimacy, a sense of military and economic power, a sense of self-confidence, self-esteem, and self-reliance all amount to a shared *common sense*. And this American commonsense is instrumental to the creation, maintenance, and reproduction of the relative inequality and powerlessness, and in some cases outright subjection, of non-American, certainly non-Western societies.

To further explicate the contribution Nietzsche makes to a conceptualization of the aesthetic dynamics of cultural identity, Ferguson invites Deleuze and Guattari into this discussion, as their discourse of "territorialization" and "coding" draws him nearer to the aesthetic formulation he pursues. With the eclipse of its constitutive other precipitated by the disintegration of the Soviet Union, the American *sensus communis* forming the infrastructure of American cultural identity weakens. America's cultural identity, whose stability depended on the potency of the discourse of morality, democracy, and selfhood fashioning the American *sensus communis*, is then set adrift, severed from the cultural terrain to which it had been moored. Thought of in other terms, American cultural identity—which had been settled on a territory that had been discursively constructed for it and thus "territorialized" by the state, its leaders, the media, corporate and other powers who mapped and co-opted, or "coded," the American cultural *sensus communis*—had suffered a "deterritorialization." Now in search of new meaning, with its deterritorialization American identity can be "reterritorialized," that is, discursively redefined. The multiple instabilities introduced by the post-Soviet era into American national and international politics created multiple possibilities for this discursive revision and reconstitution of America's cultural identity. As yet not completely settled, those possibilities eventually realized will be the work of more and less powerful state and non-state constituencies, all of whom will engage in a drawn out contest to remap, recode, and reterritorialize American cultural identity through the fabrication of new discourses. Every possibility, every territorialization realized, will carry with it a radically different set of political consequences, so the political stakes of the contestation over reterritorialization are high and perhaps as high as at any time in modern history. For in the first years of the new century, the wars being fought in and over the Middle East carry with them dramatic possibilities not only for the reterritorialization and redefinition of American cultural identity, but for the cultural identity of every world power involved.

As dire as the straits in which the world finds itself now appear to be, however, Ferguson's attempt to theorize, in aesthetic terms, possibilities for the reconstitution of cultural identity issuing both from deterritorialization and from the battle over reterritorialization, requires that we entertain positive as well as negative creative possibilities and their outcomes. What he said about the reterritorialization of American identity in the wake of the Soviet empire's collapse, may not be less true in reference to the instabilities in which the American empire now finds itself.

> The current transition between modes [of cultural identity], the period of reterritorialization, is thus a moment of relative freedom, a time that allows plural interpretations that can call into question both the fading and emerging normative standards. (*PJ*, 58)

Ferguson's argument precisely expresses the aesthetic moment in Nietzsche's thought. Nietzsche's aesthetic celebrates the sheer plurality of possibilities for cultural creation and redefinition. The politics of a Nietzschean aesthetic looks not only to the flourishing of such possibilities, but also to how we might help such possibilities to flourish. A Nietzschean aesthetic insists on the recognition and promotion of cultural pluralism by all cultures, on every culture's mutual respect for every other culture's self-understanding and efforts at self-creation, and on the critical self-understanding by every culture of how its own identity represses external as well as other internal possibilities for cultural creativity except those that conform to the narrow range of its own cultural identity. Through Nietzsche, it is clear that Ferguson has been able to move his argument from the level of culture and its politics to the level of world historical culture and world politics, which in the global era is the arena in which all possibilities for cultural creativity ultimately lie.

If the Nietzschean critique of how the *sensus communis* circulates through the construction of American cultural identity alerted us to the dangers of universalism in Kantian aesthetics, the critique of claims to universality intensifies in the congenial relationship Ferguson discovers between feminist and Wittgensteinian aesthetics. Like Wittgenstein, feminist theory and feminist politics have argued persuasively against the possibility of a "universal aesthetic," Ferguson explains. Neither is sympathetic to the belief that there is an objectively true aesthetic value or that aesthetic truth belongs to works of art that speak to the human condition writ large. For its part, feminist theory attacks the idea that all subjects enjoy a common epistemological condition allowing such insights into universality and truth. It stresses to the contrary the effect of varying social conditions on judgments, the political implications of the relation between social situation and judgment, the hostility to politics implied in a universalist aesthetic, and contests the notion that there can be any circumstances under which perception can be neutral. Gender is at work in all perception and judgment, with dominant genders dominating perception and judgment, as the male construction of women surely proves. As gender is indeed ubiquitous in all relations between subjects and objects, the hegemony of maleness also subordinates women's roles in judgment and naturalizes gender inequality to immunize the hegemony of the male gender against political challenge. And male hegemony makes a mockery of the proposal that commonality ought to be the preferred criteria for valid judgments since the hidden assumption of commonality is gender inequality and the disenfranchisement of one gender's contribution to shared agreement. While carefully summarizing the objections to a universalist aesthetic generally characteristic of feminism, Ferguson just as carefully highlights a critical implication of this work that spoils the possibility that a feminist aesthetic *as such* might appear to be the goal of feminist theory. Feminist theory's critique of the hegemonic determination of judgment belongs to a broader theoretical understanding of the situatedness of judgment, which, as Ferguson rightly points out, supports a defense of plural sources of judgment no less than plural theoretical perspectives on judgment.

Wittgenstein's agreement with feminist theory's basic principles is clear; though by bringing them into alignment Ferguson underlines the theory's aesthetic properties. As he puts it succinctly:

> The situational nature of feminist aesthetics has multiple Wittgensteinian resonances. Wittgenstein,of course, insisted on the conditionality of all judgments, and argued that the attempt to construct a universally harmonious theory of aesthetics is doomed to failure. (*PJ*, 85)

By concurring on the contextual and thus plural character of judgment, Wittgenstein and feminism multiply the possibilities for judgment consistent with a community composed of a plurality of cultural groups, all of whom exercise judgments originating in their own cultural contexts or in contexts they partially share with other cultural groups.

With their common emphasis on the contextual determination of meaning, Wittgenstein and feminism also necessarily reject the idea of a neutral aesthetic language, because, to paraphrase Nietzsche, the judgments of a cultural group are *their* judgments and necessarily so, given the contextual nature of their thought and action. This leads to a final area of agreement between Wittgenstein and feminist theory. To say that meaning is the consequence of judgments is to empower those who occupy the same cultural context to affirm what they mean in what they say, in their judgments, in other words, which likewise affirms the integrity of a culture and its right to reproduce itself over time. I should not fail to add that Ferguson's intention to dramatize the aesthetic dimensions of feminist thought by detailing its resemblance to Wittgenstein's aesthetics does not obscure their differences. And the most important of these differences is the feminist politicization of judgment. Not only does meaning vary with context, but the subjects who *construct* meanings vary with context, as well and most importantly, for neither do all subjects and their judgments count equally nor do all subjects have an equal chance to speak and to be heard.

To this point, I have reviewed the main lines of argument in Ferguson's attempt to assemble the components of an aesthetic theory that revalues judgment and its constitutive connection to the ways individuals and groups create and recreate, produce and reproduce their identities and their cultures, the very lifeblood of their existence. Ferguson marshals a Kantian, Nietzschean, and Wittgensteinian aesthetic to better grasp the vital connection between judgment and how, in a word, identities and cultures *live*. To Ferguson's mind, each offers an archetypal form of aesthetic theory—and surely he is correct in this view if we were to include not only those aesthetic features of their work he mines, but also others that have led political theory in important new directions. Of course, Ferguson's interest is not in the archetypes of aesthetic theory per se, but rather in contemporary political theory's development of a theory of judgment that takes as its point of departure Kant, Nietzsche, and Wittgenstein, who together form the tradition of thought that has contributed most to recent thinking about judgment.

So when Ferguson traces out the legacy of Kant's, Nietzsche's, and Wittgenstein's aesthetic theory in contemporary political thought—which is an important part of his project that I only briefly mention here—he turns to Arendt, Bourdieu, and Foucault, for whom a theory of judgment is a prominent concern. Despite serious problems in Arendt's work to which Ferguson is fully attentive, he admires her concept of an intensely agonistic public sphere where autonomous individuals debate political differences and arrive at an "uncoerced *sensus communis*." By persuasively arguing that judgment cannot be separated from relations of domination, Bourdieu's contribution to a theory of judgment is rooted in a concept of structural constraints that aggressively challenges the Arendtian ideal of the autonomous individual who enters into agonistic struggle to arrive at agreed upon judgments. While Foucault, on the other hand, who appears to be Ferguson's strongest theoretical ally, is suspicious of the very notion of commonality for the threats it poses to the freedom of those whose own differences lie outside the realm of judgment most likely to issue in commonality. Such points as these only hint at Ferguson's sense of how contemporary political theory has productively incorporated the tradition of aesthetic theory he has examined.

To enter further into this and other aspects of Ferguson's discussion exceeds the purpose of this introduction, which must be limited to showing how the problems on which he has worked open to a consideration of James's pluralism. What is far more interesting to report by way of conclusion is his recommendation about what, in the final analysis, ought to be contemporary political theory's future relationship to the tradition of thought that bears on the aesthetics of judgment.

> The most obvious question left concerns the possibility of a synthesis of all three positions—the Kantian, Nietzschean, and the Wittgensteinian—in a contemporary theory of aesthetics. But I am unconvinced that this is the right question for this project, or even a particularly important one. What is important about these theories of aesthetics is not the eventual commingling of each into a grand theory of aesthetic unification, but in the questions they raise. (*PJ*, 132)

So what are the decisive questions these positions raise for contemporary political theory? For Ferguson, the overriding question concerns the possibility of what he refers to as a "dissident aesthetics." A dissident aesthetics proceeds from the understanding that no matter how ideologically or structurally constrained individuals or their groups are by the networks of social life in which they are implicated, they remain architects of a world bounded by those limits and have available a vast range of judgments through which they can resist and revise relations of domination. Opportunities for judgment not only survive the impositions of constraints, but those constraints also create new sources from which judgments can be formed. Judgment is irrepressible because, whether free or not, and flowing from every source productive of judgment, its plurality is irrepressible. It is the plurality of opportunities for judgment that makes the aesthetics of judgment universal.

The differences or areas of agreement on the aesthetics of judgment there are among Kant, Nietzsche, and Wittgenstein. Arendt, Bourdieu, and Foucault are secondary to the river that runs through them, the idea of plurality as the irrepressible font of human experience, which in different forms has surfaced time and again during the course of this discussion. Aesthetic theory appears to be inseparable from the question of plurality to which it leads. It is this connection between aesthetics and plurality that invites consideration of the pluralist theory of William James, whose advanced understanding of pluralism will move the aesthetic turn in contemporary political theory forward, as it also enables political theorists to conceive of pluralist politics in other new ways.

—Morton Schoolman,
State University of New York at Albany

## Notes

I am grateful to Jon Sisk and Michael McGandy of Rowman & Littlefield for their continued support of **Modernity and Political Thought** and for their thoughtfulness and professionalism, which make it possible for this editor and authors alike to produce their best work. And while each of the authors in this series will earn rewards and punishments commensurate with his or her own contribution, they are the hidden architects of the series and each must share credit with me for developing **Modernity and Political Thought**.

1. William E. Connolly, *The Augustinian Imperative: A Reflection on the Politics of Morality*; George Kateb, *Emerson and Self-Reliance*; Stephen K. White, *Edmund Burke: Modernity, Politics, and Aesthetics*; Tracy B. Strong, *Jean-Jacques Rousseau: The Politics of the Ordinary*; Thomas L. Dumm, *Michel Foucault and the Politics of Freedom*; Michael J. Shapiro, *Reading "Adam Smith": Desire, History, and Value*; Richard E. Flathman, *Thomas Hobbes: Skepticism, Individuality, and Chastened Politics*; Jane Bennett, *Thoreau's Nature: Ethics, Politics, and the Wild*; Fred Dallmayr, *G. W. F. Hegel: Modernity and Politics*; Seyla Benhabib, *The Reluctant Modernism of Hannah Arendt*. With the exception of Benhabib's work, published in 2003, all new editions were published by Rowman & Littlefield in 2002.

2. Kennan Ferguson, *The Politics of Judgment: Aesthetics, Identity, and Political Theory* (Lanham, MD: Lexington Books, 1999).

3. For example, see *The New Pluralism: William Connolly and the Contemporary Global Condition*, edited by David Campbell and Morton Schoolman (forthcoming from Duke University Press, Spring 2008).

# Preface

WILLIAM JAMES DID NOT DIE A PRAGMATIST. Today he is known for the refinement and popularization of pragmatism, the theory of truth as arising from and answering practical needs. But at the time of his death, in 1910, James enjoyed both academic and popular fame. He was recognized for his contributions to psychiatry, for his acceptance of mysticism, for his anti-imperialism, for his attacks on racism, for his muscular pacifism, for his anti-vivisection writings, and for his pluralism. James remains well known, and even widely read, but little of his reputation outside psychology and pragmatism remains. While many of his ideas have been integrated into mainstream thought (or made less relevant by the passage of time), his pragmatism remains alive precisely because its challenges to received theories of truth remain as fresh as ever.

For these same reasons, our inheritance from James should include his creation of pluralism. Pluralism, even more than pragmatism, comprises his most important legacy. His pluralistic concepts stand central to issues of state (and nonstate) institutions, personal and social identities, and international relations. His perceptions about plurality in our creative methods, intellectual understandings, and conceptual limitations remain unparalleled. Yet the intellectual history of Jamesian pluralism, both here and abroad, has been poorly understood until today.

James found in plurality the desiderata of meaningful life. Those who attempted to discover the deep universalisms of experience or to overcome variety as troublesome (including present-day thinkers who may call themselves "pluralists" but treat political differences as regrettable realities) aimed, in James's vision, to impose their ideals on others. Writing against the dominant

"Hegelianism" of philosophy, with its assumptions that the purpose of thought lay in the discovery of the absolutes of truth, society, and selves, James attempted to discover and celebrate the ramose and divergent strains of being that make up knowledge and experience. Sometimes contradictory and sometimes parallel, for James these streams comprised the very stuff of individuals, of nations, and of thought itself.

This attention was driven in part by the era in which James lived. Before the advent of the state-sponsored twentieth-century horrors of fascism and totalitarianism, James found the rationalization and systematization of the modern world profoundly destructive of humanity. He recognized their appeal: the human impulse toward security and certainty leads away from the reality of destabilizing differences. But unlike many who followed him, his fellow pragmatist John Dewey included, James harbored a fundamental suspicion of the governmental inclination toward these standardizations. States, he held, deeply oppose the diversity of experience, and thus he rejected their study (which was soon to congeal into the category "political science") except where it negated this diversity. A Jamesian outlook, in other words, resists the practices of statecraft and sovereignty so dear to political science, and instead suggests a variety of experiences and subject-positions. In this, James provides defense against and guidance through the demands of modern autocracy, both at the levels of the self and of institutions.

Pluralism is thus fundamentally connected to politics; indeed, pluralistic approaches reveal the very project of Hegelian centralization, whether philosophic or statist, as political. Yet James's inception of pluralism remains generally forgotten and its implications ignored, especially in political debates. While the importance of pluralism has been continuously debated over the past century in philosophic, political, and practical circles, James's name has been notably absent from virtually all of these.

Part of the reason for this absence is James's outsider status in political philosophy. Unlike Hegel, Marx, or Nietzsche, each of whom analyzed the contradictions of modernity, James fits uneasily into the history of political theory. Occasional incursions are made on his behalf, by the likes of Richard Rorty or Cornell West, but even then, he is represented as merely one of three loosely affiliated pragmatists. Additionally, his writing sits uncomfortably with many of the philosophic ideas for political thinkers: the absolutism demanded by Kantian or Hegelian thought was anathema to James. His opposition to unity (of selves, communities, and even thought) disturbs the accepted projects of most political philosophy, where the universally just, equitable, and stable political situation remains the implicit ideal.

This arises precisely because James's writings were profoundly engaged by and responsive to the people and world around him. In his psychology, he recognized that the concept of a unified self contradicts itself, that the situation of the self in the modern world is necessarily multiple. And it was to those selves that he addressed himself, writing for philosophers and for citizens, for his enemies (with whom he was generous), for his friends (with whom he was anti-totalizing), and for himself (with whom he was confrontational).

Three important themes of Jamesian pluralism weave through this book. Explaining its intellectual foundations and development makes up the first and most important theme. For James, the universe is not, as its name implies, unitary; for this reason he often referred to the "multiverse" or the "pluriverse." He argued that it—and we—operate on multiple registers, wherein locations, times, spaces, and approaches position and compose our interactions, our experiences, and even our truths. Chapter 1, "The Universe and the Pluriverse," shows how James's philosophy leads to endless variety replacing ontological surety.

The theoretical implications of this insight bind closely to its political potentials. Contrary to those who think that the purpose of philosophy should be to develop a teleology of ideology and action to be discovered and followed (Hegel served as this kind of foil for James), a Jamesian pluralism rejects the feasibility and desirability of this kind of approach, contending that such attempts always result in exclusions, marginalizations, and subjugations. The impetus to develop the absolute or the whole enforces the partial—which we can never exceed—on those whose parts do not fit. This approach also means that exclusion is never complete, that difference is never absolute, that outsiders are never fully exterior. Pluralism attends to connections where absolutism sees only disunity. Those with whom one disagrees, it turns out, may have something important to say, even if one is not ultimately convinced.

James preferred stories to directives, listening to telling, and self-criticism to critique. He opened himself up to these possibilities, interrogating his own presumptions and foreclosures while being influenced by other perspectives. Many of these investigations led to his extraphilosophic fame, encouraging him to write and lecture expansively, beyond the boundaries of the academy. Through pluralism, James found the possibilities of war in peace, of oppression in democracy, of sickness in health, and of life in death. These implications have been the most readily lost from popular and academic conceptions of pluralism.

This book's second theme, developed in the second and fourth chapters, addresses the intellectual histories and trajectories of pluralism since James's time. Chapter 2, "The Descent of Pluralism," examines the reformulations and changes to political pluralism from James's time to the late twentieth century. Picked up from James by the political and social theorists Laski, Figgis, and Cole, the term *pluralism* was used and misused by Hsiao and later by Dahl and

Truman. Each of these stages, in its own turn, arose from attempts to politicize pluralism, but each also formalized and enfeebled it. By the time pluralism became a descriptive category for political scientists, it had fallen from its prescriptive Jamesian roots to a normative, universalizing justification for state power.

The theme of pluralism's intellectual histories and trajectories reemerges in chapter 4, "*La Philosophie Américaine.*" Challenging the accepted contention that foundations of European and American philosophical traditions are oppositional, this section traces the qualitative influences and derivations of Jamesian pluralism in Europe. Though most philosophers think of James as an eminently American theorist, a thorough investigation of his influences, and of those he influenced in turn, ties him closely to European thought, especially that of his contemporary Henri Bergson. Inasfar as Bergson and James exemplify the foundations of European and American philosophical traditions, the putative opposition of these traditions is illusory. To speak of "American" as antithetical to "Continental" philosophy ignores and obscures their equally important commonalities. It also, not accidentally, constructs an intellectual lineage of purity, uncontaminated by multiple streams of thought.

This book's third and final theme concerns the redemption and reinvigoration of Jamesian pluralism for contemporary theoretical, ethical, and political issues. One immediately apparent parallel with today's public debates arises from the role that James's anti-imperial stance played in his pluralism, and vice versa, as discussed in chapter 3, "Sovereignty, Self-Determination, and the Nation." James's pluralism and his activist opposition to the emergent United States Empire developed coincidentally—not to say as happenstance, but rather in the sense of mutually constitutive progressions. James championed "the many" in philosophical terms and equally advocated the rights of peoples to control their own destiny; these intellectual developments fed one another. Thus, for James, a people like the Filipinos had the right to create their own political system and country, as they best saw fit, not one according to the United States's desires and needs.

Chapter 5, "Onticology Recapitulates Philosophy," takes up Jamesian pluralism as a different way of looking at things. Physical things are generally seen as outside of philosophy, or as examples for or correlatives to it. For a pluralist, however, things make up philosophy. As central to experience, things create the worlds around us. But things can never be universally, fully appreciated: Perceptions, as Kant pointed out, cannot exceed the limited and partial. Thus, we need a pluralistic theory of things, especially for those (such as those engaged in object-oriented computer programming) who must theorize things at abstract levels.

Taken together, these themes reconfigure William James as a philosopher not of pragmatism but of plurality. Jamesian theories, in their political, social, and empirical implications, lead away from the confusion of the self with the world, indeed from the conception of selves and worlds as unified. They lead away from utopias, from the ideology of the pure sovereign, from the confusion of logic with force.

Is it possible to learn from William James? James's universe is not ours, true. But neither was it his—nor is ours ours—for universes cannot be thus constrained. To attend to the ways pluriverses exceed those within them is also to consider the ways incommensurate times, spaces, and bodies overlap and influence one another. To pluralize is to insist on the irreducibility of connections, the excess of the world, and the creativity that arises from learning and responding rather than consolidating and securing. To pluralize is to rescue selves from individuals, histories from History, theology from alethiology. To pluralize is, in short, to learn ways to exist as human beings who engage the world rather than always trying (and always failing) to conquer it.

# Acknowledgments

ANY AUTHOR CONCERNED WITH PLURALISM, at least by the sorts of pluralism that William James's philosophy encourages, must recognize peculiarities arising from the act of writing. For even when a book is composed by one person, certain aspects of it—what that person thinks, how that person lives, and who that person is—fundamentally depend on other people. Those people's ideas, their values, their histories, and their cultures all help construct the author's interests, passions, and approaches. Our worlds arise from interactions with others' worlds.

This is not necessarily strictly a question of influence and imitation. In fact, as James reminds us, the people responsible may even be those who we most overtly fashion ourselves against, those whose ethical commitments and conceptual demands we most resist. Others serve as intellectual inspiration, even if we have never personally met those individuals. And still others actually participate in the acts of creation—suggesting, editing, correcting, questioning, and critiquing. As the final group is easiest to thank, I would like to offer my appreciation to as many as I can remember (though I am also indebted to those who antedate me in arguing that James's work has an intrinsically political component: Robert L. Beisner, Frank Lentricchia, George Cotkin, and Joshua I. Miller).

Work by Richard Flathman (*viz.*, his book *Reflections of a Would-Be Anarchist*) started me down the path of thinking seriously about James beyond his pragmatism. For helping me work through the shape and purpose of the overall project from its origination, I thank Timothy Kaufman-Osborne, Lee Mitchell, and William Connolly. Chapter 1 was encouraged and critiqued by

Michael Gibbons and Steven Johnston. I profited greatly in the second chapter from comments from Cheryl Hall, Lee Mitchell, and Irma Levomäki. The third was inspired and analyzed by Kathy Ferguson, Fred Dallmayr, and José M. Rosales. Michael J. Shapiro, Suzanne Guerlac, and the many interlocutors of the William James listserv contributed to chapter 4. The fifth arose from a discussion instigated by Jane Bennett and continued by Thomas L. Dumm. To each of these engagées I offer my sincerest gratitude.

Morton Schoolman, the editor of this series, has helped direct and encourage the book for the past three years; his patience and close appraisal have made this project possible. I am both proud and pleased to join the company of previous authors. Michael McGandy, his counterpart at Rowman & Littlefield, has ably stewarded the manuscript through its final stages. Also important were two way stations: an earlier iteration of chapter 3 appeared in *Beyond Nationalism? Sovereignty and Citizenship*, edited by Fred Dallmayer and José M. Rosales (Lanham: Lexington Books, 2001). A shorter version of chapter 4 appeared in *Theory & Event*, V. 9, N. 1 (2006). My thanks to Lexington and The Johns Hopkins University Press for reprint permission. I also relied on the often-invisible institutional networks which allow scholars access to difficult-to-find articles and books; without the Los Angeles Public Library system and the University of South Florida Library (and their respective librarians) I could never have written this book.

Finally, three particularly heartfelt acknowledgments, each of which arises from the pluralistic entanglements and credits that arise within the lives of academics. First, to Carolyn Eichner: She has been copyeditor of, and constant companion to, this book. Her support, love, and critical perspective have clarified both the historical implications and components of pluralism. Second, thinking deeply about the pluralistic sources of the self leads one to contemplate one's own past: My parents, Dick and Jean Ferguson, themselves seek out new experiences and people, as well as enthusiastically engaging otherness. The family they created, including my sister Rona, has allowed for and encouraged me in my explorations. Finally, my intellectual and pedagogical commitments have been formed in response to inspirational teachers. At the top of this list are Thomas L. Dumm, Kathy E. Ferguson, and Michael J. Shapiro, each of whom has led by educational, authorial, and ethical example. My thanks to all who have formed my personality and my thought—credit and guilt binds to each of you.

# 1
# The Universe and the Pluriverse

WILLIAM JAMES DISCOVERED UTOPIA IN 1896, when he visited the Assembly Grounds at Lake Chautauqua in Western New York. He found the town of Lilydale perfectly designed: satisfied adults and families engaged in exercise, popular lectures, and excellent health facilities. There were institutions of learning from kindergarten to college, and learning itself was held in high regard. In short, it was a community of "[s]obriety and industry, intelligence and goodness, orderliness and ideality, prosperity and cheerfulness."[1] Facing the twentieth century, James had found an alternative to most cities: a place free of disease, hatred, and strife, and filled instead with unfettered thought, humanistic concern, and brotherly fellowship.[2] Yet by the end of a week, James recounts, he could think of nothing but leaving.

He had begun to feel the perfection of Lilydale weighing heavily upon him, and he yearned to escape once again to the malevolence and intensity of the outside world. Without the tribulations usually faced on a daily basis, he had discovered, life became uninteresting and bland, and ultimately not worth living. Indeed, it was only upon leaving the Assembly that he was finally able to appreciate the Emersonian heroism of the people all about him—those who toiled, labored, and struggled against the very evils that Chautauqua had succeeded in casting away. This overall experience led James to remark on the paradox of disappointment with perfection: How is it that one can be so profoundly unsatisfied with the fruition of one's own ideals?

James's critical analysis of Lake Chautauqua was not based on the usual criticisms of political utopianism: that its architects err profoundly in their assumptions as to what people want, for example, or that utopias can never exist due to the fundamental selfishness of humanity. The ideals of the Assembly's founders coincided fully with those of James and he quickly praised the features of life he discovered there. Nor did he intimate that these particular aspirations are misguided; in fact, he termed Lilydale a success. James initially extended his stay at the grounds from a day to an entire week because he found the atmosphere so salutary; he is given, "in effect, a foretaste of what human society might be, were it all in the light, with no suffering and no dark corners."[3]

Far from criticizing the particulars of the utopianism he encountered, James found that the overall achievement—the institutional and blueprinted fulfillment of his own stated ideals—to be spiritually enervating and personally disappointing. Instead of elevating the human psyche, he determined, the embodiment of perfection deadens it, primarily because such an existence leaves no place for the dissension and friction that ultimately gives life significance.[4] This recognition served as a synecdoche for the direction his philosophical work would increasingly take. James's evolving interest in the concepts and implications of human difference would ultimately lead him to conclude that such difference is central to human identity and happiness. James thus formulated an immensely influential philosophical precept, one at least as important as his better-known refinement of Pierce's "pragmaticism." James called this concern with human multiplicity "pluralism," and it was to effect great changes in twentieth-century philosophy and politics. He defined pluralism in a deliberately extreme form (one that would be increasingly moderated by those influenced by his thought in the future): that central, fundamental difference is crucial to human existence.

## Why Pluralism?

James's empiricist tychism contrasted radically with previous philosophies. Resolutely nonmetaphysical, it also included the possibility (even the desirability) of religious faith. Meant as experimentally descriptive, it was also intended as a profound warning about the rapidly increasing appetite for homogeneity at the turn of the century. Thoroughly rigorous as a philosophy, it was also proposed as a publicly accessible one. Like Dewey after him, James determined to avoid the abstractions and convolutions that made philosophers like Kant and Hegel virtually unreadable to a general audience.

James's philosophy argued for an embrace of fundamental multiplicity. His last major work, entitled *A Pluralistic Universe*, arose from a lecture series he gave in England.[5] In it, James censured "our" (philosophers' and others') tendency to fall into what he called "idealistic monadism": that is, to hierarchize entirety over partiality, to think of the whole as the natural, highest conception.[6] James identified this propensity as the most pernicious of all philosophical tendencies, and also as the strongest impetus in the history of thought. The proclivity to totalize is, he argued, the cornerstone of virtually every attempt to build a philosophical system, but is also the reason each system so poorly corresponds with everyday empirical reality. Such theories (or, more properly, metatheories) are intrinsically anti-empiricist, arising from preconceptions about reality that everyday life is then modified to fit.[7] James argued instead that there would likely "ultimately never be an all-form at all, that the substance of reality may never get entirely collected, that some of it may remain outside the largest combination of it ever made. . . ."[8]

For James, the problem of "the one and the many" stood as the most important of all philosophical problems. Unfortunately, he argued, philosophers had historically sacrificed the pragmatic realities of the human world to idealistic monism. In doing so, they had promoted the proclivity of the modern world toward a unitary, homogenous mass. "We found colonial, postal consular, commercial systems, all the parts of which obey definite influences that propagate themselves within the system but not to facts outside of it."[9] The result, James argued, is "innumerable little hangings-together" of previously independent parts, parts which are increasingly caught up in the machinery of the modern.[10] James noted the proclivity of philosophy to tie these parts together tightly, to force a unified meaning from the vast array of meanings, operated in a way complicit with the forces of the modern world.

James contended that unifying all of these meanings into one meaning would lessen, not strengthen, our understanding of reality. Even early in his works he examined the plurality of meaning that humans (and nonhumans) can derive from the same systems. In *Principles of Psychology*, his first major work, he described how each person takes from "mere matter" particular, distinct perceptions. "My world," he explains, "is but one of a million alike imbedded, alike real to those who may abstract them. How different must be the worlds in the mind of eel, cuttle-fish, or crab!"[11] But James's pluralism does not lead to a relativistic inability to defend particular lives. The worlds in which crabs and cuttlefish live are real, very real, to those aquatic creatures; that they are radically different from ours, and in most ways incommensurate with our own, in no way implies that their world (or ours) do not matter in the most material and elemental ways. Nor does it point toward solipsism and isolation, what James dismissed as "absolute pluralism." The mere realization of such differences between these worlds does not mean that we can then reject any of them out of hand.

Even though James dismissed the idea that intellectual inquiry will result in a unified theory of things, pluralism did not reject attempts to bring together multiple meanings. James carefully distinguished his radical pluralism from isolationism and solipsism. Understanding how the world's various parts correlate is important, but not more so than understanding how they differ; the goal is to comprehend both. Such a goal does not lead to meaninglessness, as those who see *pluralism* as synonymous with *relativism* would hold, but rather to parallel meanings. James did not deny meaning, nor did he hold that meanings are entirely man-made. Meaning can even come directly from objects themselves. "Things," he argues, "tell a story.... Retrospectively, we can see that altho no definite purpose presided over a chain of events, yet the events fell into a dramatic form."[12] But, he continued, such meanings are not universal. "The world is full of partial stories that run parallel to one another, beginning and ending at odd times."[13]

James did not entirely discount the possibility of relativism, but he found such a possibility not only unthreatening to politics and philosophy, but ineffectual. Unions between people might very well be, under the most rigorous of philosophical definitions, illusory; however, James pointed out, this makes them no less real. Connections between people are concrete and substantial insofar as they *seem* concrete and substantial; in "a world where both the terms and their distinctions are affairs of experience, the conjunctions which we experience must be at least as real as anything else."[14] James thus rejected Berkeleyan doubt about personal connection. Though a purely experiential empiricism could lead to radical skepticism, James's version emphasizes that the reality of our relationships with others and with things trumps purely intellectual doubt. Whether or not incommensurability is a epistemological fact holds far less importance than the reality that it is pragmatically transcended.

Indeed, it is this incommensurability that leads us to the realm of freedom. When we are determined by our philosophies, our countries, or our psychologies, we cease to be involved and intellectually stimulated beings. When, on the other hand, we encounter varieties (be it of cultures, modes of thought, or religious experience), we become engaged by the uses and choices of those variations. If one true way actually existed, as in Hegel's idealism, the idea of human freedom would perish.

James presciently recognized that plurality and complexity would be central motifs of the twentieth century. He saw the pluralism he so valued as threatened by modernity and the tendency to unify. James considered such centralization inimical to freedom itself; unification by its very nature forecloses the possibilities that are central to human liberty. James's pluralism arose from a suspicion "of groups themselves and particularly of theories and doctrines that privilege groups philosophically, surround them with special legal and political protections, and promote their dominance in social and political life."[15]

James's philosophy and his politics shared a central tension: the conflict between, on the one hand, the creation and valuation of difference and, on the other, the existence of (and people's preference for) systems that demand unity. Philosophy and politics both required, from his perspective, the attempt to take proper account of the shared senses of lived experiences and to the unalterably separate nature of these experiences.[16] It is in this respect that James's radical pluralism has been central to political questions of the twentieth century—and it is in this role that certain contemporary theorists have begun, once again, to maintain the value of a radical pluralism, though often without James's name attached.[17]

Most of the aspects of Jamesian pluralism were well known to both the turn-of-the-century public and James's scholarly contemporaries. But over the years, James has become known to most academics as merely the middle figure in the pragmatic triptych of Pierce, James, and Dewey. James's politics and public influence generally disappeared; his cultural impacts are attributed more to his popularization of pragmatism than to any particular philosophical creation. Pluralism itself has fared even worse. In contemporary political philosophy, it usually stands for little more than a set of institutional methods to apportion and control carefully categorized variations in a larger state system. Most recent political theories of pluralism accept difference as a necessary evil, an unfortunate aspect of the human condition that often necessitates amelioration. They differ as to whether it is best relieved by legal means, by the direct involvement of governmental agency, or by the establishment of institutional mechanisms; but the overall goal, for most, is the camouflage or dissolution of disagreement. Few join James in celebrating the existence of these differences and in looking for ways to further establish a variety of experiences.

The history of this shift from Jamesian pluralism to today's pluralism provides the subject of the next chapter. But it is important here to briefly describe the vast gulf between the two versions. James's pluralism considered alterity necessary to any being or system's growth, transformation, or self-analysis. The pluralism of the late twentieth century—of those calling for "pluralist forms of law" or hoping to transform other countries into "pluralist democracies"—is a formal pluralism: a systematization of rules meant to mitigate differences and establish a centralized unity (law, policy, and so forth) through which conflicts can be dependably resolved.

This latter conception relies on a severe impoverishment of plurality, positioning difference as exclusively organizational, that is, as consisting of "autonomous organizations within the domain of a state."[18] Distinctions become organizationally bounded. Disputations become problems to be solved and thus ended. Any kind of deviation from established norms fits into one of two categories: either the normative/organizational (which thus becomes, in Jamesian terminology, immaterial and "toothless") or the perverse/seditious (and thus necessary to eliminate from the bounds of the political).

Political disputes, consequently, tend to be about how to move from the latter to the former. That which is outside the boundaries of politics seeks to move within them, where—under the institutional teleology of institutional pluralism—they will be absorbed into the body politic. Inside, they merely pose problems to be solved; outside, they may be safely annihilated, demonized, or ignored. Profound dissidence (or dissidents) can only hope to become normative/organizational problems, which may lead to certain problems being "solved" without posing a challenge to an overall normative and organizational structure.

Questions regarding the rights of gays and lesbians present a contemporary political example of how this parsimonious sense of plurality limits political discourse. Such an impoverished politics implies the binary question of "Are 'homosexuals' (assumed to be a consistent and harmonious category) an interest group that needs and deserves a metaphorical 'seat at the table' in politics, or are they a mortal threat to the homogeneity of the body politic that must be eliminated or at least silenced?" If the former, then gay politics becomes merely a novel but familiar strain of political discourse: what rights are available and which should be acknowledged (for example, should gays and lesbians be allowed to marry)? If the latter, then a self-normalizing majority can expel mention of homosexuality from all proper institutional channels (schools, mass media, ratings boards), and thus protect children and other innocents from moral decay and corruption. Thus the current interpretation both presupposes the concreteness of categories and transforms challenges to normativity into preconceived institutional polemics.

Neither of these two conceptions encourages a Jamesian reading of difference; the norms of heterosexuality never come into question, and each position reinforces the conviction that sexualities are austere and secured. What would a pluralism that raised substantive rather than procedural issues look like? It might encourage doubt about the dualisms between homosexual and heterosexual identities. It could provoke investigations of those mechanisms which preclude self-awareness of "inappropriate" desires. It may imply that a zero-sum conception of love, care, and sexual attentiveness itself limits our abilities to relate to other humans. Conceivably, it could lead not only to an increased understanding of how straight culture differs from gay culture, but also how gay male culture differs from lesbian culture, or even exposes us to the varieties, ambiguities, and complexities that exist within each ostensibly singular culture. Jamesian pluralism, in other words, unsettles assumptions and categories, allowing for self-investigation, generosity, and critical engagement.

Is this an absolutist insistence on pluralism, as the wearisome objection from univeralists would have it ("Aha! You are really insisting that everyone be a pluralist, which is itself a kind of universalism!")? Not at all: James recognized that few saw the world as he did, and he hoped that they would not. Utopias like Chautauqua, after all, are boring. Instead, James offered his own point of view as an invitation, as an engagement. Not that he would fail to draw conclusions from his pluralism: as the third chapter will discuss, he declared the United States's emergence as an imperial power a moral disaster, as the U.S. government justified its oppression and murder of subject peoples on the grounds that they were not enough like us.

James did not limit this combination of respect and pluralism to an interest in international state affairs. To him, the political tendencies toward monism were as strong within the United States as elsewhere. Indeed, he saw the two as inextricably linked: as the modern world underwent constant and increasingly unitary systematization, individuals within that world endured ever more strict mandates for homogeneity.

A few examples from James's pen follow. James vocally criticized lynching, the conspicuous, brutal underpinning of Jim Crow. He shared the familiar liberal horror at the illegality and immoral racism of such slayings. But James went further, equally disturbed by any collective justification of socially condoned killing, where "the murder is regarded as a punitive or protective duty."[19] It is here, he argued, in the unification of violent actions with communal justification that "the peril to civilization is greatest."[20] The centralization of moral approbation, in other words, itself does violence to social relationships.

James also strongly opposed the centralization of medical authority, in his time evidenced by the movement to institutionalize and certify mental health practitioners. Even though he actively disliked those who would try to heal clients under the banner of psychology, he argued that to legally limit experimental inquiries to licensed doctors would confine intellectual progress and would "be a public calamity."[21] James even supported views directly at odds with his own regarding psychology. Although he believed Freud to be monomaniacal, "obsessed with fixed ideas," and ridiculous for his focus on dreams, James nevertheless hoped, as he wrote in a letter to Théodore Flournoy, that Freud's followers would take Freudian ideas "to their furthest extremes."[22] Thus the encouraged overlap between generosity and pluralism: How many academics wish to see their opponents' ideas reach full fruition?

Perhaps James's most notable willingness to try to understand difference came from his empathy with crusades he opposed. His 1910 essay-in-leaflet-form, "The Moral Equivalent of War," was emblematic of this ability: In this work, James, a self-professed "pacificist," showed exceptional empathy, verging on sympathy, for the militaristic viewpoint. In the midst of an antiwar polemic, James reminded his audience of the ways in which militarism has a moral center, one of sacrifice and honor and valor.[23] Though he ultimately rejected this morality, he recognized the sway that military symbolism held at the turn of the century and he entreated other pacifists to build alternative sites of patriotism and veneration.

In each of these cases James found it not only possible but necessary to look beyond his own beliefs, his own most treasured aspirations for humanity, in order to understand where they conflict with others' ideals. He wanted to see ideas with which he disagreed fully realized; he did not merely hope for people to understand views that conflicted with their own, but to actually hope to see those other views actualized. He urged those who agreed with him to see their own shortsightedness. This kind of pluralism arose from not only a true commitment to the possibility of forms of difference but also a recognition of the legitimacy of those forms.

These recognitions emerged not, as might be expected, from James's well-known pragmatic critique of truth as partial and contextual, but instead from his related emphasis on the necessary coexistence of different kinds of religious faith. Personal religious faith held primary importance for James; it gave both meaning and structure to his life.[24] But unlike the religious leaders of his time (or our own), James recognized that his faith was, if not partial, at least personal. He asserted that others had equal claim to religious faith—claims often notably dissimilar to his own. Religions, while plural and often contested, also have the power to bridge difference. James argued that the most important political aspect of religion was the "social appeal for corroboration, consolation, etc."[25] His theory of religion, thus able to negotiate both commonality and incommensurability, was replicated in his later philosophy.

This form of pluralism differed dramatically from later conceptions that emerged from "political science." A radically pluralistic universe cannot support a universalist conception of power. But how can there be politics without the reified construct "power"? For James, the negotiations of commonality and diversity, of identity and difference, take place not through relations of power but in "networks of acquaintance," strong relationships that hold among people and things.[26] These networks—examples of which include friendship, acquaintance, knowledge, and detestation—continue onward beyond the people and things so held, to connect the individual to other parts of the world. Power and commonality, argued James, are traceable in "lines of *influence*."[27]

With the exception of a very few contemporary philosophers, these Jamesian ideas no longer appear in political theory, though the term *pluralism* certainly does.[28] What, then, of the supposedly political aspects of the pluralism that emerged at the end of the twentieth century? As liberalism has grown into the dominant, even exclusive, political paradigm in the United States, it has incorporated bits and pieces of other theoretical traditions, including pluralism. Many liberals, from Berlin to Oakeshott to Rawls, have considered pluralism a prominent component of their liberalism; a liberal society, they have argued, cannot exist without coming to terms with its structural diversity. Yet their *liberal pluralism* and James's *radical pluralism* are distant cousins, at best.

## James against Liberalism

In recognizing the legitimacy of other people, beliefs, and countries, James seemed to many to be a part of mainstream liberalism. But while Santayana's contention that James "shared the passions of liberalism" may be arguable, to call James a liberal misleads.[29] Liberalism contains an implicit teleology of collective normativity that Jamesian pluralism eschews. For liberals, respect for other people or for other countries points to a greater good, where mutual consideration and tolerance together lead to peace. But this aim is notably absent within James's philosophy: after 1898, he rarely prescribed how other nations should behave. By not exhorting particular actions he faced criticism by those who believed philosophy should have normative ends. This led A. J. Ayer to criticize James for making "no ontological decisions at all."[30]

The putatively pluralist liberalism that emerges through the course of the twentieth century accepts and even celebrates the plurality of individuals, groups, and cultures while still simultaneously subsuming that plurality in the systematic boundaries of a civil society. Liberalism looks to establish rules by which a society can act, in Rawls's terms, "fairly"; it strives to negotiate difference and incommensurability in a way that treats everyone according to an overarching sense of impartiality. Isaiah Berlin's pluralism, for example, does little more than support his liberalism, a liberalism that provides the playing field upon which different interests can negotiate. Berlinian pluralism, as I argue in the next chapter, accepts the state as the necessary negotiator of competing interests, and thus privileges political forces over other sources of self-identity.[31] For Berlin, the final goal remained the resolution of profound differences. Berlin thus rejected James's pluralist challenge to the self, the constant interrogation of one's very nature. Compare, too, Michael Oakeshott's rendition of *lex*, the system of mutual intelligibility underpinning any civic community, however diverse.[32] Such a system allows, even readily admits, difference, but it must ultimately be made intelligible via the mechanisms of law and politics. The boundaries thus drawn are expansive, larger than traditionalists would wish—but they are still drawn in indelible ink.

What happens to those creatures that are judged deficient in their intelligibility, or those that transgress these boundaries, or those who understand but ignore them? This includes the traditionally and contemporarily problematic categories of slaves, women, criminals, the insane, and children, each of whose inclusion and exclusion from intelligibility and political involvement has been contested. Liberalism, in its various forms, always gives the following answer: they are removed from the bounds of the political, where they no longer cause political trouble. This excision can be done violently, legally, rhetorically, philosophically, or by combining these methods. However it is done, it involves the denial (1) that these "sorts" of people can participate in politics, and (2) that liberalism itself has had any part in constituting these typologies. Ultimately, liberalism attempts to solve the problem of sameness and difference by expanding the definition of sameness but continuing to rely on the exclusion of difference.[33]

In contemporary theory, John Rawls best expresses the liberal perspective of pluralism. Pluralism is, in his words, "a fact"; liberalism's responsibility is to deal most humanely with the difficulties this fact engenders.[34] This kind of pluralism is plainly institutional: the objective is to create governmentalities that can either negotiate the claims and counterclaims that plurality creates, or that can declare certain of these claims alien to civil society and prohibit them.[35] At best, liberalism can only produce a purely descriptive form of pluralism where the plurality of human experiences (often falling under the rubric of "culture") are mere givens. This kind of pluralism argues that humans will always be different and the realities of political life force us to accept this. But a Jamesian radical pluralism is more prescriptive and less sanguine. Namely, it encourages intellectual and political differences, recognizing those alternative worlds as necessary to life's vitality. For James, pluralism is prescriptive; for Rawls and other liberals, it is descriptive.

Even in its most positive renditions in contemporary politics, pluralism itself rarely means more than the ability to join associations of individual interest (for example, Michael Walzer's rendition of pluralism as "critical associationalism"[36]). Such a reading not only impoverishes pluralism but also diminishes our understanding of James himself. It enables contemporary commentators, self-described pluralists, to view James as primarily cultivating the ability of an individual to join new, though preexisting, alliances "while remaining associated to all the other groups to which she belongs."[37] Such pluralisms not only institutionalize difference and deny that individuals are constituted within networks of meaning, but also mitigate the meaning of conflict. Rather than a potentially self-changing experience, it becomes merely a dispute between two sides.

An often subterranean (but sometimes overt) fealty to universalism haunts liberalism: Human rights may take shape, for example, because of the liberal requirement that all humans be more alike than not, that they share an essential humanness. Even though that humanity must be shored up, defined over and over, readjusted every time abortion-inducing medications or genetically identical sheep or chess-playing computers come along, the liberal outlook holds fast to the ideal that humanity is an ultimately solid foundation. Liberalism declares a deep-down level of mutuality; this is a form of idealism to which, say, Kant subscribes but James does not.

And this is because, for James, the relationship across difference does not absolutely require objective measures of worth and equality. People and their dogs, James points out, can have complex, loving, and mutually giving relationships even through their mutual unintelligibility; "we to the rapture of bones under hedges, or smells of trees and lampposts, they to the delights of literature and art."[38] Yet the two can love one another, trust one another, and depend upon one another.[39] For James, relationships exceed formal recognition or explicit systematization; even though the dog and the human are not within the same objective framework, there can be love, trust, and engagement.

The value in this relationship escapes liberalism: liberals hold that without equivalence and formal equality, both of which rely on deep levels of mutuality, true relationships do not exist. Dogs cannot be liberals. Short of expanding the definition of "the human" to include animals, things, and nature, liberalism cannot comprehend political relationships beyond the boundaries of the human.

What, then, can contemporary politics take from Jamesian pluralism? In part, that multiple ways of knowing, living, and experiencing do exist. But this is common knowledge, taught by pluralism in all its forms. What has been forgotten since James—and what an engagement with James can remind us—is how these different epistemological forms profoundly affect one another; that they hold intrinsic value for that very reason; and that the contestations that result do have and should have the power to transfigure us. James knew that the structures of logic, whether formal or more traditionally philosophical, deny these implications because rigid distinctions—for example between "things" and "people"—form the groundwork upon which logic rests.[40] But a radically pluralist outlook can perceive these boundaries as both challenges to and necessary components of selves. A Jamesian can thus look for ways to encourage and foster difference rather than following liberalism's lead by treating it as a philosophical chimera, something to fear, avoid, and attempt to bypass, unscathed.

## Notes

1. William James, "What Makes a Life Significant," original lecture given at Bryn Mawr in 1892 and published in 1900 (New York: Henry Holt and Company); reprinted in *Talks to Teachers on Psychology and to Students on Some of Life's Ideals* (Cambridge, MA: Harvard University Press, 1983), p. 152.

2. James neglects to recount that Lilydale was perhaps the most internationally visible site of spiritualism, founded and persevering to introduce the outside world to the wonders of connection with the next world. This is especially interesting given his later concern with the relative nature of spiritual truth.

3. "What Makes a Life Significant," p. 153.

4. James readily admits that he lifts this integral concept from Tolstoy, whose *War and Peace* and *My Confession* James cites at length. See "What Makes a Life Significant," pp. 157–58.

5. Attendance for this lecture exceeded the attendance of any previous lecture series at Oxford. See Stanley A. Mellor, "Pragmatism at Oxford," *Boston Evening Transcript* (Nov. 4, 1908), p. 18.

6. The book originated in a series of lectures given at Oxford (Manchester College). See *A Pluralistic Universe* (Cambridge, MA: Harvard University Press, 1977). Pages 25–62 pay particular attention to the evils of monism.

7. Though James accuses empiricists of being as duped by monism as rationalists. See *Pragmatism* (Cambridge, MA: Harvard University Press, 1975), p. 65.

8. *A Pluralistic Universe*, p. 20.

9. *Pragmatism*, p. 67.

10. *Pragmatism*, p. 94.

11. *Principles of Psychology* (Cambridge, MA: Harvard University Press, 1981), p. 277.

12. *Pragmatism*, p. 70.

13. *Pragmatism*, p. 71. James serves as a curious precursor to contemporary theorists of objects, from Arjun Appadurai to Bruno Latour. These latter theorists, however, insist on the social assemblage of these stories, whereas James the individualist would hold that people can themselves discover these stories. See chapter 5.

14. *The Meaning of Truth* (Cambridge, MA: Harvard University Press, 1975), p. 64.

15. Richard Flathman, *Willful Liberalism: Voluntarism and Individuality in Theory and Practice* (Ithaca, NY: Cornell University Press, 1992), pp. 7–8. Yet even Flathman, one of the most eloquent of the few who champion James as a political theorist, argues that "it is too much to say that social, moral, or political plurality are indispensable to James's ideal" (p. 69). Flathman, however, identifies pluralism with the dynamics of associational action: In order to be meaningful, Flathman argues, such a plurality must also be social. James the individualist would certainly disagree with this assumption, as do I. As even a cursory glimpse of, say, gay and lesbian autobiographical literature shows, identities at odds with dominant cultural norms need not be shared by others to be both personally and politically meaningful, no matter how personally rewarding such sharing may be.

16. See "A World of Pure Experience" in *Essays in Radical Empiricism* (Cambridge, MA: Harvard University Press, 1976) pp. 21–41.

17. In the United States, the term "pluralism" has fallen into disfavor, mostly because of its twentieth-century history; even those closest to James tend to avoid it. See chapter 2.

18. Robert Dahl, *Dilemmas of Pluralist Democracy: Autonomy vs. Control* (New Haven, CT: Yale University Press, 1982), p. 5.

19. "A Strong Note of Warning Regarding the Lynching Epidemic," *Springfield Daily Republican* (July 23, 1903), p. 11; reprinted in *Essays, Comments, and Reviews* (Cambridge, MA: Harvard University Press, 1987), pp. 170–73 (quotation, p. 171).

20. "A Strong Note of Warning," p. 171.

21. See his March 24, 1984 letter to the *Boston Evening Transcript*, reprinted in *Essays, Comments, and Reviews*, pp. 56–62.

22. Letter to Théodore Flournoy, Sept. 28, 1909, *Letters of James and Flournoy*, p. 224.

23. "The Moral Equivalent of War," in *Essays in Religion and Morality* (Cambridge, MA: Harvard University Press, 1982), pp. 162–73.

24. See, generally, *The Varieties of Religious Experience* (Cambridge, MA: Harvard University Press, 1985). In making the idea of immortality the motivating force in belief in God, see p. 412.

25. William James, *Writings, 1902–1910* (New York: Library of America, 1988), p. 1183.

26. *Pragmatism*, p. 67.

27. *Pragmatism*, p. 66. This phrase echoes many years later by Deleuze and Guittari's "lines of flight." Deleuze and Guittari are, I think, Jamesians within contemporary philosophy; the reasons for this are discussed in chapter 4. The central questions of *A Thousand Plateaus*, for example, are those of multiplicity, assemblage, and the tendencies toward mastery (what Deleuze and Guittari term "microfascisms"). See *A Thousand Plateaus: Capitalism and Schizophrenia*, trans. Brian Massumi (Minneapolis: University of Minnesota Press, 1987).

28. There is an obvious correlation between James's radical pluralism and many contemporary philosophies of politics, culture, and meaning. Particularly noticeable is the work of William Connolly, who has recently been investigating pluralism, in part through the lens of James. See *Pluralism* (Durham, NC: Duke University Press, 2005) Prior to this, Connolly was arguing for "pluralization" (a term specifically distant from "pluralism") in *The Ethos of Pluralization* (Minneapolis: University of Minnesota Press, 1995). In continental philosophy, see Deleuze and Guattari's espousal of "rhizomatics" over "arboreality" in *A Thousand Plateaus*—a profoundly Jamesian project. Michel de Certeau's recently translated political writings also bespeak radically multiple sites of meaning-creation, meanings that make a monadic incarnation of power impossible. And Jean-Luc Nancy's advocation of a "generosity of *ethos*" over an "ethic of generosity" seems taken directly from James's playbook. (See Jean-Luc Nancy, *The Experience of Freedom*, trans. Bridget McDonald [Stanford, CA: Stanford University Press, 1993], p. 146.) Though none of these European authors credits

James as a forebear, the links between James, Bergson, and Continental philosophy will be explored in chapter 4.

29. George Santayana, *Character and Opinion in the United States, with Reminiscences of William James and Josiah Royce and Academic Life in America* (New York: C. Scribner's Sons, 1920), p. 91.

30. A. J. Ayer, *The Origins of Pragmatism: Studies in the Philosophy of Charles Sanders Pierce and William James* (London: MacMillan, 1968).

31. It is John Gray's *Isaiah Berlin* (Princeton, NJ: Princeton University Press, 1996) that most encourages grappling with the pluralist tendency in Berlin. Against Gray, I argue that Berlin has always been far more concerned with finding a neutral space for the contestations of human diversity than with celebrating that diversity itself, that is, ultimately he values liberalism over pluralism. Gray argues that Berlin reverses this hierarchy, and is willing to jettison liberalism when it comes (as it must) into conflict with pluralism. I think Gray's interpretation of Berlin is wrong, but his arguments have their allure.

32. See *On Human Conduct* (Oxford, UK: Oxford University Press, 1975), pp. 147–58.

33. The most rigorous and extreme liberalisms maximize sameness by abstracting humanity beyond the boundaries of located identity. Michael Sandel's critique of Rawls's attempt to do this, specifically of Rawls's "original position," is properly devastating; the insistence on the part of communitarians that we are always established within various communities is convincing. Yet the communitarian solution to this conundrum, namely, that we must thus turn to the building and policing of a commonality, is more oppressive and pernicious than the original difficulty.

34. John Rawls, *A Theory of Justice* (Cambridge, MA: Harvard University Press, 1971).

35. This criticism I take from Michel Foucault's essay "Governmentality" in *The Foucault Effect: Studies in Governmentality*, ed. Graham Burchell, Colin Gordon, and Peter Miller (Chicago: University of Chicago Press, 1991).

36. "The Civil Society Argument" in *Dimensions of Radical Democracy: Pluralism, Citizenship, and Democracy*, ed. Chantal Mouffe (London: Verso, 1992), pp. 89–107.

37. Avigail Eisenberg, *Reconstructing Political Pluralism* (Albany: State University of New York Press, 1995), p. 61. To be fair, Eisenberg ascribes this philosophy to both Dewey and James, but it strikes me as equally inadequate with regard to Dewey, though for different reasons.

38. "On a Certain Blindness in Human Beings," *Talks to Teachers . . .* , p. 133.

39. I expand on James's reading of dog love in "I ♥ My Dog," *Political Theory* 32, n. 3, pp. 373–95.

40. *A Pluralistic Universe*, p. 116.

# 2

# The Descent of Pluralism

> It is but the old story, of a useful practice first becoming a method, then a habit, and finally a tyranny that defeats the end it was used for.
>
> —William James[1]

WILLIAM JAMES POPULARIZED THE TERM *pluralism*. The word, infrequently used prior to James's *fin de siècle* writing, has since taken on a life of its own, especially within the confines of political thought. And like all lives, this one has moved away from its origins over time. James created pluralism as an anti-Hegelian distrust of all universalist systematizing—an anti-teleological ethos that emphasizes the profound and meaningful differences in the worlds of different people. In short, James's pluralism was *prescriptive*.

Over the course of the twentieth century, however, the term *pluralism* came to primarily mean something far different, something merely *descriptive*. Pluralism is now understood as referring to the fact of human difference, the unpleasant and sometimes unavoidable incommensurability of values that threatens people's abilities to build political institutions, share meanings, and even communicate. Discussions of pluralism now focus on the difficulties of overcoming the distinctions that it highlights. Pluralism, in other words, has been shifted from a promise to a problem.

This chapter explains how this contemporary meaning has evolved over the course of a century. From the state-centric pluralism of Laski, to the pluralist universalism of the unjustly forgotten Hsiao, to the strictly formal pluralism of Dahl, pluralism was slowly stripped of its specific prescriptive qualities. James saw pluralism as an aspiration, an experiential stimulation beyond the usual narrowness of human existence; for mid-century political science, it had become a troublesome "fact" which a properly constituted state could mitigate. Even for Isaiah Berlin, one of the best-known late-twentieth-century pluralists, the world's multiplicity represented a dilemma rather than an aspiration. As institutionalized "pluralism" (which remains firmly lodged within current political conceptions) abhors fundamental difference, perceiving heterogeneity as a threat to community, it is only by understanding and rejecting this conceptual impoverishment that contemporary politics can return to an engagement with pluralism.

## Against Hegel

By James's death in 1910, the tenets of his public philosophy had entered both popular and academic understandings of politics. But it was James's championing of pluralism that established it as a central issue in political theory (especially Anglo-American political theory) for decades to come. Just as James's conceptions of pragmatism led John Dewey to a lifelong concern with the public nature of philosophy, so did his pluralism influence a new generation of political scholars.[2] Yet this political form of pluralism became increasingly domesticated as it became allied with the conflict between partisan politics and policy. Although the ascent and development of pluralism in the twentieth century is a familiar story within American political theory, I want to retell it, but not—as is usual—as the gradual purification and refinement of a theory based in interest group politics as objects of scientific inquiry. Instead, I argue, the history of political pluralism is one of increasing justification for normative enforcements and collective valuation, a trajectory implicitly antithetical to the philosophical vision from which it arose. Each form of pluralism subsequent to James, which I call, in turn, "anti-Hegelian," "formalist," and "institutionalist" pluralism, stretched further and further from the kind of pluralism James had envisioned. Each form therefore also increasingly lost the philosophical underpinnings that made his principal focus on difference so radical.

James did not originate the theory of pluralism. He readily acknowledged his indebtedness to the German anti-Hegelian Gustav Fechner.[3] Both the Polish Nietzschean Wincenty Lutoslawski and the German legal scholar Otto von Gierke had used the term to describe their own philosophical systems. It is also likely that Proudhon, Hume, Renouvier, and Ménard contributed to James's pluralist epistemology.[4] And James had contemporaries who were reputable pluralists (in practice, if not in name): the well-regarded English jurist Frederic Maitland and the long-obscured Arthur Bentley.[5] But it was William James whose public standing and philosophical expertise brought theories of pluralism, and the term itself, to a central position in the era's philosophical thought. By popularizing philosophy and insisting on its necessary relation to significant social issues, James led the way for the empirical development and focus that political theory, in the garb of pluralism, would take through the twentieth century.

Jamesian pluralism first helped fashion the thought of a notable group of anti-Hegelian political philosophers: Laski, Figgis, and Cole. Harold J. Laski's influential 1917 *Studies in the Problem of Sovereignty* specifically used James as the inspiration for an anti-Hegelian conception of politics.[6] Laski agreed with James that the common philosophical assumption of a goal of political wholeness is an intellectual chimera, and is ultimately detrimental to political culture. The search for unity, Laski argued, should be replaced by a "perpetual question mark, the sense that unity is a concept introduced by the unifier."[7] Laski used a vast array of such question marks to criticize the tendency of institutional and political organizations to aspire to ideal forms, forms which then attempted to fit all people and institutions into their own Procrustean restrictions. Ultimately, Laski rejected the commonplace assumption that the proper locale of power is the state, which acts as a central, compulsory, and unifying site of political power.

The most overt philosophical target of Laski's pluralism was Hegel's conception of the unified state as the foremost and proper location for engaged human life—what Laski referred to as the Hegelian assumption that the state was "not only the culmination of the social process, but the embodiment of the highest purpose humanity could know."[8] State-centered politics, Laski argued, impoverished political activity, since those who do not meet the requirements of the authority (be that a party, a faction, or a king) will always be cast out. Even in the best cases, where a national government attempts to meet the requirements of the majority of its citizens, there will be citizens whose needs and desires stand in opposition to the majority. For Laski, true state sovereignty, the centralization of all legitimate power in one person or structure, cannot and should not exist.

Laski contended that no one social grouping should automatically take precedence over others, regardless of the powers it might accrue to itself; thus he overtly termed his theory a "pluralistic theory of the state."[9] Laski presupposed that all people had a variety of collective allegiances: associations, corporations, or trusts. He pointed out that assuming that one of these actually controls all legitimate forms of authority and violence leads to a profound misunderstanding of power. If such a state, "absorptive in a mystical, Hegelian fashion," were possible, it would be the ultimate in tyranny. But one need only look at the profound limitations on state power in associative life to note that no such empire could exist.[10]

Yet our assumption that such a powerful state does exist leads to dangerous misunderstandings. For Laski, people naturally tend to assume the increasing centralization of authority. "The only hopeful way of breaking down this inertia," he argued, "is by the multiplication of centers of authority." Ultimately, Laski was a radical federalist, arguing for the opposition of power at the very heart of a state: "the secret of liberty is the division of power. [T]hat political system in which a division of power is most securely maintained is a federal system."[11] By separating the power of a state against itself, Laski contended, states' tendencies toward universalist claims to power could be minimized though never conquered.

Laski referred to William James to justify his federalism, though James himself had used the term *federalism* strictly metaphorically. When Laski wrote "We find the state to be, in James's phrase, distributive and not collective," he referred to terms James had used to describe states of the lived world, not states of the international community.[12] But as justification for his theories against sovereignty and for federalism, Laski continued to refer to James through his intellectual career, even defending *A Pluralistic Universe* to his close friend Oliver Wendell Holmes (a strong James critic).[13]

Laski was joined in this critique by other less politically oriented but still influential English pluralists writing in the period immediately following World War I. Though primarily historians rather than political philosophers, J. N. Figgis and G. D. H. Cole shared with Laski an overwhelming rejection of the state as the unifying force in social relations. Though they did not use the term *pluralist* to describe themselves, and though neither Figgis nor Cole focused on developing overtly systematized philosophies, the three together came to be known as "the pluralist school."

Figgis, like James, was interested in how a variety of spiritual beliefs provide political and moral heterogeneity within society.[14] When a church (in his primary example) incorporates as an association, it creates a particular set of rules, standards, and organizational structures for its members. All of what he calls "corporations," public or private nonstate associations, have these specific requirements, which depend on the group's autonomy. They are not outside the law, precisely, but neither are they of it: A church's rules are not de facto legal rules and should not be determined and constructed by the state.

Even the largest association, Figgis held, should not be a fundamentally political one, but a social one. The famed "Commons" is not in fact the state, or even the association of all the people, but rather the "community of the communities."[15] For Figgis, the multiplicity of organizations to which people belong, not their nation-states, fashion who they are, and attention must be paid not to "the people" but rather to their various groupings. By emphasizing the abilities of nonstate organizations to determine their own aims, methods, and rules, Figgis intended to show the relative unimportance of the state in our public (that is, collective and associative) lives.

G. D. H. Cole's focus on guild socialism went even further, causing him to altogether reject the state as even the coordinator of social and economic organizations.[16] Self-created and self-sustaining guilds of workers, Cole held, should determine their own autonomous systems of governance and punishment. When recompense or amerce is called for, the guilds, not the state, should mete it out. Cole contended that guilds properly recognize specific, limited aspects of human life and thus act properly to represent their members.

The same cannot be said for states. Even in representative systems of governance, Cole argued, proper representation cannot take place. Representation can only exist for specific purposes in specific contexts: He considered the assertion that an agent can epitomize any citizen's various interests in general to be absurd.[17] Like Figgis, Cole asserted that the variety of associations within society held greater importance than the particular members of a society; unlike Figgis, Cole viewed the state as intrinsically corruptive of the authority of other forms. Contrary to Figgis's assumption that states and alternative loci of power could happily coexist, Cole saw state power as intrinsically competitive with other forms of power. For Figgis, churches and states could coexist easily, whereas Cole's socialism condemned the state's intrinsic disempowerment of workers.[18] Cole asserted that states would always view guilds as antagonistic and would see guilds' attempts to create elective power structures as a usurpation of governmental power. More than Laski or Figgis, Cole's criticism of sovereignty rejected the very legitimacy of a state, bringing him close to an organizational anarchist position.

Together, Laski, Figgis, and Cole provided the intellectual basis for what they intended as a politicization of pluralism. Each strongly criticized the then-prominent Hegelian assumption that a single, centralized authority constituted the distinctive mark of a modern society. By showing, as Laski did, that revolutions could (and did) happen even when authority seemed strongest, the pluralists demonstrated the limitations of centralized power and emphasized the alternative resources available to resist political forces.[19] In his own way, each of these thinkers enlarged the Jamesian vision of pluralism by examining how human differences—differences that could be discussed empirically and historically—undermine the tendency toward unity.

Yet for this group of pluralists, the ultimate goal of a pluralist politics differed from James's overall celebration of dissimilarity: For them, pluralism predominantly aimed to contest state absolutism. By emphasizing social structures other than the state, these pluralists stressed how different kinds of institutional and informal groups could lay claims to political power, claims previously dismissed by those whose Hegel-infused theories continued to privilege statist interests above all others. Early pluralists did hew rather closely in one regard to James's conception of radical difference, specifically in their denial of "the integrating function of the state."[20] Yet the overall aim of pluralists such as Laski, Figgis, and Cole was securing alternative ways to establish the representation of nonstate interests. Indeed, by his later work, even Laski was calling for more specific and formal alternative forms of political organization: advisory councils, community committees, and other types of substate actors.[21] Put simply, Laski's federalism became more important than his pluralism. He and his fellow pluralists increasingly developed a state-centric conception of plurality; the politicization of pluralism ironically enshrined the state at the center of the philosophical questions they raised.

### The State of Pluralism

John Dewey is generally considered William James's foremost intellectual successor, and is well recognized as a public philosopher in the United States. But Dewey's attitude toward pluralism was overtly lukewarm, both in theory and in practice. Where he brought pragmatism to play in the societal sphere, he rejected much of what James had found valuable about human difference. Take, for example, Dewey's aversion to American cultural pluralism: "I never did care for the melting pot metaphor, but genuine assimilation to *one another*—not to Anglo-Saxondom—seems to be essential to an America."[22] Dewey did not ascribe to a predetermined universal type for Americans (namely, he did not hold that all must emulate Anglo-Saxon culture), but did assert assimilation as the primary goal of society. He wrote, "The way to deal with hyphenism [German-American, Jewish-American, and so on] . . . is to welcome it, but to welcome it in the sense of extracting from each people its special good, so that it shall surrender into a common fund of wisdom and experience what it especially has to contribute."[23] Indeed, much of Dewey's intellectual and political work toward what he called the "common interest" presumed a unified public.[24]

Even those who did argue for pluralism—James's more direct successors—continued to change the meaning of the concept. By the period preceding World War II, pluralism had moved even further from James's vision. Though Kung Chuan Hsiao is best known today (if he is known at all) as the intellectual link between Laski's generation and that of the mid-century pluralists, Hsiao's redefinition of pluralism was central in bringing pluralism into the service of the state. He began the mammoth project of establishing the coexistence of pluralism and sovereignty. Rather than reject statism out of hand, as his predecessors did, Hsiao attempted to reconcile the demands of legal institutions, centralized government, and a diverse people. Arguing that legal pluralism, whatever its history, is inherently unstable and has ultimately "no law at all," Hsiao asserted instead that a centralized legal system should regulate and direct the conflicts that arise from a pluralistic society.[25]

In this conception, Hsiao provided a new template for pluralism, one that recognized diversity and plurality within experience, but aspired to see those variations as part of a greater unity: the state. Unlike any of his pluralist predecessors, for whom particularity trumped unity, Hsiao was "eager that the particulars shall, at least ultimately, be capable of resolution into a universal."[26] He defended, for example, the concept of a Rousseauian "general will" as the practical goal of pluralism; the conflicts that a plural society generates arise from differences in how to realize the general will. Every clash, therefore, "should result in some profound harmony of wills." Irresolvable conflicts, according to Hsiao, foretell the "final disintegration of society itself."[27] Hsiao's form of pluralism openly rejects the desirability of true divergence; in his reading, unlike that of his predecessors, radical difference does not enhance human experience but threatens it.

Why, then, did Hsiao call himself a pluralist at all? What remained of the pluralist project in Hsiao's recasting? Hsiao jettisoned the promotion of pluralism as an objective: It was, he argued, ultimately inimical to the necessary unity of an ordered state. However, he retained the particularly descriptive powers of pluralism: both its ability to depict the quotidian realities of politics and its ability to portray how cooperative projects can emerge from different sources. Jamesian pluralism, he noted, characterizes humans as part of many different projects and "hangings-together"; with this, Hsiao happily concurs. But he roundly rejected James's insistence that such differences make human lives meaningful. Such divergences should be allowed to stand against *one another*, according to Hsiao, but if they are permitted to stand against the centrality of law, then sovereignty itself is called into question.[28] While Hsiao viewed James as the founder of pluralism, he also criticized James's ideas as a threat to law and community. For James, Laski, and Cole, pluralism constituted an alternative to the centralization of state power; Hsiao, by contrast, made pluralism safe for the state.[29]

Hsiao's revamping strongly influenced other pluralists of the time. Writing toward the beginning of World War II, Henry Meyer Magid reinterpreted pluralism as being primarily "a philosophy of freedom," concerned with the ways in which citizens within a democracy can control the "operations of their government."[30] Though Magid primarily addressed the history of political pluralism, his focus repudiated the anti-statism of his forebears, instead sanctioning the state's ability to protect individual freedoms. In criticizing the earlier pluralists, for example, Magid accused Cole of failing to address politics at all, assuming that only political parties (which Cole dismisses, like he dismisses representational democracy) engage in politics.[31]

Magid intended to rescue the concept of sovereignty from previous pluralists, positioning his and Hsiao's as *concrete pluralism* in contrast to Laski, Figgis, and Cole's *abstract pluralism*.[32] Instead of looking at the government of the state, Magid argues, proper political theory should consider the government of the community, which "needs ordering."[33] For both Hsiao and Magid, the central concern remained that of freedom. But this freedom was no longer found in rejecting the role of the state, but rather in aspiring to a state able to juggle the array of interests that comprise modern democratic society.[34]

## Fixing Pluralism

By the middle of the century, pluralism had descended to a plea for the state to negotiate competing interests. The previous enmity between pluralism and statism was disregarded, replaced by a pluralism that facilitated state power. Pluralism was reduced to a formal and institutional instrument, now seen by political theorists such as Robert Dahl and David Truman as a constitutional arrangement balancing powerful political groups against others.[35] More concerned with "the balance of power" than with any sort of epistemological plurality, these institutional pluralists discussed how interest groups within a constitutional republic reached an overall equilibrium, whereby various claims made by one group are reinforced, channeled, and contested by other groups. This rendition of pluralism is thus concerned with the negotiations of power between competing interests, especially insofar as these require a negotiator, viz, a constitutional state. The state, no longer repudiated, became a necessary entity, namely, the mechanism used by these competing groups to help recognize their self-interest.[36]

To recent generations of political theorists (though not necessarily philosophers), therefore, pluralism has focused on issues such as party affiliation, interest group dynamics, judicial maneuvering, and coalition politics. Racial, economic, gender, class, and cultural associations are described monolithically, with little attention to their historical formation, internal fault lines, and interrelationships. And the formal mechanisms of government are understood to be the most important, if not the only, locations in which politics takes place. When, to take a recent example, Samuel Huntington argued that plural "civilizations" are doomed to clash, or that people whose ancestors arrived from Mexico inherently differ from the rest of U.S. citizens and thus will never become true Americans, he drew implicitly on this latter conception of pluralism. What, he asked, should the role of the U.S. government be when confronted with these unassimilated (and inassimilable) peoples?[37] Those who respond to him accepting his categorizations often reinforce his assumptions, even if they disagree; the very groundwork on which contemporary pluralist debates takes place reinforces the reification of identities and politics.

This focus on the mechanistic aspects of power and the reification of political interests into interest-group policy battles, and cultural identities into solidities of competing identities, stands considerably distant from James's ideas. For where James encouraged the provocations that come from a pluralistic universe, the pluralism of Dahl and other formalists concerned with political unity in a fragmentary polity was an entreatment for stability, for the circumscribed and calculable securing of political identities.[38] Dahl, for example, saw pluralism's goal as the necessity of keeping a nascent majority fragmented to prevent it from uniting against a minority.[39] Truman, similarly, explicitly denied the need to explain the preexistence of social groups, arguing that they have always existed; indeed, he went so far as to state that "all groups are interest groups because they are shared-attitude groups."[40] Thus, he argued, society works best when such groups are in equilibrium. Such theories depend on three central premises: a securely circumscribed sense of identity such that "majority" and "minority" remain appreciable, a sense of groups as intrinsically oppositional, and a greater interest in the stability of the state than in democratic majoritarianism. The necessary and sanctioned role of the state, for the formalist pluralists, was the safe-keeping of political identities by providing a guarded structure to minimize conflict. This form of pluralism thus replicates the Hegelian relationship of subject to state "by reaffirming the investment of its multiple subjects' political identity into formal avenues of participatory citizenship."[41] Multiple organizations, therefore, even help to minimize the necessity of state action by serving to "create mutual control"; a pluralist country need not even be bothered by its own multiplicity.[42]

By the latter half of the twentieth century, theories of pluralism were no longer resources against the centrality of the state in modern political life. Instead, they aimed at developing social equilibrium, a political state of rest in which each demand from each interest group could be subsumed into the larger social entity. Pluralism had become a realm of political theory where the presupposition of unity overwhelmed difference; where, in Henry Kariel's blistering criticism of pluralism, the "assumption of an underlying harmony of parts is placed beyond challenge, and social scientists are steadily led toward a theoretical scheme, a constitutive order, which will finally synthesize all conflicting social units."[43] James's radical pluralism, in other words, had entirely disappeared: the tendency toward monadism that pluralism was meant to remedy had claimed pluralism itself.

The reliance of Dahl, Truman, and their followers on such formalist conceptions provoked serious criticisms, severely weakening the plausibility of what by then counted as pluralism. C. Wright Mills excoriated them, convincingly arguing that such a political theory disregards the ability of a certain societal component to overwhelmingly set the terms of debate.[44] Kariel criticized them for the extent to which "pluralism is in effect hypostatized" and thus naturalized and made apolitical by such a theory.[45] For Kariel and other critics of formal pluralism, Dahl and Truman employed it to strengthen and legitimize the power of a state against its own dissidents, rather than encouraging or even allowing dissidence.

Many of the offshoots of this formalist pluralism were even more intellectually and empirically suspect. For example, W. J. Mackenzie's self-ascribed pluralism aimed at properly dividing "politically uncivilized" peoples in order to arrive at certain simplified representations.[46] Such peoples, who erroneously saw themselves as united, needed to be split into opposing groups to hasten their political development. Such "pluralist" divisions, not coincidently, pointed toward the necessity of continued dominance by colonial powers over those who united against their oppressors.

Even those who seemed to embrace contention in political affairs did not encourage it beyond particularly constrained boundaries. For Hannah Arendt, who in many other ways seemed to encourage a pluralist outlook, political activity remained profoundly limited by her insistence that it follow formal rules of public action. Arendt's celebration of agonistics appears to embrace a kind of Jamesian pluralism until one notes how she constrains and limits actual contestation by her distinctions between public and private actions. This is not a minor point, as some who champion Arendt would have it: Arendt's theoretical limitations disallow in vital ways the three major American-European political movements of the late twentieth century (racial equality, feminism, and gay and lesbian rights). For example, Arendt criticized the use of children and the informed law-breaking that characterized the American civil rights movement in her "Reflections on Little Rock."[47] By positioning civil rights as a "political" issue, and excluding children from the realm of public actors, Arendt attempted to philosophically delegitimize the political actions that brought about civil rights in the United States.

Isaiah Berlin, perhaps the best-known late-twentieth-century philosopher to address pluralism, agreed with James that no one way of looking at the world can (or should) trump others. Berlin's "value incommensurability"—the recognition that multiple moral and cultural goods and obligations may be irreconcilable, even for one person—formed the foundation for his pluralism that allows for human differences.[48] He reintroduced pluralism as central to philosophical investigations of ethics, politics, and the ontological status and empirical reality of human existence.[49]

Berlin's importance within philosophy rests in large part on his insistence that pluralism is unavoidable and that no universal moral order exists that can ultimately be decoded through reason (a critique he ultimately attributed to the romantic tradition).[50] And though he rarely directly cited William James, his assertions of the world's great multiplicity reflected Jamesian intent. Like James, he emphasized the partiality of human understanding, the experiential nature of moral acts, and the ultimate undecidability of differing outlooks.[51] Berlin, too, rejected the Hegelian insistence that reason will naturally lead to a universal systematization: It is not only wrong but dangerous. Though Berlin's investigations and conclusions, like James's, were couched in the language of philosophy, he also recognized his conclusions as important to politics and policy. As many commentators have pointed out, Berlin's thought emerged in opposition to the twin monisms of communism and fascism, systems which in spite of their substantial differences shared an ideology of unity. For both, the role of politics was to purify society of its deformities, of those individuals who did not or would not understand that the greatest happiness rested in the full unity of the people. Berlin detested any structure which positioned "freedom" (what he called "positive freedom") as the purification of difference—that is, which insisted that humans be coerced into ideals, and be stripped forcibly of their actions and opinions which keep them "blind, or ignorant, or corrupt."[52]

A philosophical or political approach must therefore take into account the natural human variety found among any population. Take for example the following quotation:

> The ultimate fact of the variety of human nature, our differences of both hereditary capacity and social nurture, this is inescapable. . . . But equality does not mean identity of treatment. It implies an insistence that there is no difference inherent in nature between the claims of men to happiness. . . . It implies an attempt to give each man a chance as similar as possible to those of other men to utilize what powers he may possess.[53]

For Berlin, the fact of human differences demands a variety of methods for living life; the insistence that one set of *oughts* can serve all equally is not only theoretically wrong but an imposition by one set of peoples onto others. But it may come as a surprise to those familiar with Berlin, that though the above quotation sounds precisely like him, it is actually the words of Harold Laski, circa 1930. In many ways, Berlin returns to a form of English political pluralism with a new terminology of the political.

Philosophers have attacked Berlin's value pluralism for decades. Their reproaches sound much like those who criticized James. The cavil: Berlin's commitment to negative liberty is a transcendent valuation, which logically contradicts his pluralism; all moral theories, they then conclude, must be foundationalist.[54] But while Berlin's approach has a Jamesian cast, using James's language, Berlin also calls for a kind of *dis*engagement with difference. For Berlin, the negative liberty of being "left alone" is fully sufficient. Unlike James's insistence that the exorbitances of the world demand a growth of the self, that the multiplicity of the universe can encourage reflection and change, Berlin's pluralism aims to allow others to live their own lives in their own ways. Berlin ultimately calls merely for the allowance of difference, that is, tolerance. This emphasis on negative freedom omits those aspects of political encounter and contestation which James argues make us who we are; it presumes, like John Stuart Mill's plea for toleration, that true pluralism is found in detachment.[55] Rather than needing, and thus encouraging difference, Berlin, like the formal pluralists, aimed merely to learn to let well enough alone.

This is not to deny that other contemporary political theorists continue to use pluralist, Jamesian ideas, but the above history has put such freight on the term itself that few today call themselves *pluralists*. Many avoid the term because they assume it has never meant what they, like James, want to suggest. Others, such as certain European philosophers (e.g., those discussed in chapter 4), are influenced by James in ways they themselves do not even recognize. Thus, the term's original significance, its prescriptive qualities, are today almost totally divorced from it.

## Decline and Fall

There seem to be five related changes in the transition from Jamesian radical pluralism to the formal pluralism of the late twentieth century. Between them, they do not encompass all of the important shifts in the terminology of pluralism, nor are they necessarily explained by social forces external to philosophical evolution. But the developments that served to institutionalize "political science" made (and continue to make) demands on pluralism that discouraged its original purposes and encouraged its sterility.

First among these changes is the evaporation of the complexities of freedom as a constitutive purpose. For the latter-day pluralists, human freedom became a formality that demanded to be dealt with; the aim of producing freedom had entirely disappeared. Even in its most generous form, pluralism had devolved to nothing more than the lack of constraint of the self. When pluralism's foremost aspect does not exceed John Stuart Mill's conceptions of liberty, it loses its prescriptive value. James's concepts of freedom arose from the combination of engagement with otherness and a critical establishment of the self. In contrast, those who called themselves pluralists a century later aimed to minimize engagement and defend selves from the threats of otherness.

The second major shift was the expulsion of human contestation from public spaces. When negative freedom stands as the ultimate goal of political theory, agonistics (even the tightly circumscribed conflict that Arendt extolled) can do little more than impose on individuals, selves that seem to magically preexist politics. While James held contestation as a necessary requirement for the fulfillment of human character, latter-day pluralists limited it to attempts to negotiate unfortunate adversarial positions, as with competing rights-claims or associational battles over access to resources.

The third important transformation over the past century was the depoliticization of political theory. For James, the utopia of Chautauqua was perfectly attainable: its only real prerequisite consisted of the shutting out of people who would challenge its objectives (indeed, James foresaw the likelihood of such self-congratulatory isolation increasing through the twentieth century). As pluralism and political theory more generally evolved, they became increasingly concerned with ways to create smaller or larger Chautauquas, ways to minimize controversy and formalize dissent. The normative tendency in political theory has been to enable the disregarding of difference, to make it immaterial or negotiable, forgetting the ultimately antipolitical nature of such disregard.

The fourth change was pluralism's decline within an overall shift in political science toward representing political actors as economic consumers. The increasing economism of political science has meant that many of the issues of interest to political philosophers—sovereignty, legitimacy, representation—have been recast as potential choices in a marketplace of ideologies, where voter/consumers are peddled competing brand names. When difference means little more than a "rational" choice between commodities, pluralism ceases to challenge dominant formulations of political order. It instead becomes a way of organizing plurality into an ordered structure of classification, "a determinate system out of a multitude of conflicting individual wills which could be taken to be autonomous and undetermined."[56]

Fifth, and finally, the appeal of the term itself continued to grow. Though political theorists had increasingly replaced James's politicized pluralism with an anti-political liberalism, they still called such a beast *pluralism*. Indeed, most liberal countries are often referred to as being *pluralist democracies* or having *pluralist constitutions*. These countries, of course, do not foment, encourage, or attempt to develop difference; they certainly do not seek out alternative ethical or political systems in order to encourage critical self-analysis. Liberal, formal pluralism can thus trade on the appealing laudability of Jamesian pluralism without the actual peril of self-critique. Stripped of its substantive meanings, self-congratulatory pluralism can be employed to justify almost any attempt to contain disagreement within formal parameters.

Contemporary studies rarely note that the history of political pluralism has strayed so far from its original valorization of competing, alternative frameworks. When this is recognized, it is usually described as the attempt to make James's theories effectively political. Some argue, for example, that Cole, Laski, and Figgis took the stale philosophical constructions of pluralism and reinvigorated them by attending to power and politics, thus discovering the substantive significance of pluralism, or that multiculturalism, say, is the first utilitarian application of pluralism to the political realm.[57] These arguments neglect, however, the way in which James's own pluralism was consistently engaged by and formed alongside his political outlook. To suggest that political thought remained peripheral to a Jamesian sense of pluralism is to fundamentally misunderstand the various relationships between James's politics and his philosophy. Certainly he did not always reduce his political and philosophical interests solely to state-centered issues; those uses of pluralism came later and were applied more significantly by those discussed above. But he did not reject plurality as politically central to countries and their populations, to the personal, and to the international. Most importantly, contemporary analyses also neglect the contingency central to the origins of Jamesian pluralism; in their ignorance, they create a pluralism closer to the universalism antithetical to James's intent.

## Notes

1. William James, *A Pluralistic Universe* (Cambridge, MA: Harvard University Press, 1997), p. 99.

2. As for Dewey himself, his progressivism dispensed almost entirely with James's radical pluralism, instead emphasizing a common vision of the future based on the establishment of collective values. In many ways, Dewey thus returned to the aims of classic liberalism, albeit with a progressive twist. Timothy V. Kaufman-Osborn convincingly argues that Dewey's is a communal liberalism, that for him "the preeminent task of modern society . . . is the reconstruction of the shared fund of accumulated meaning." Dewey is thus engaged in the classical problems of liberalism, Kaufman-Osborn argues. See his "John Dewey and the Liberal Science of Community" in *The Journal of Politics* 46, n. 4 (November 1984), pp. 1142–65. Quotation from p. 1150.

3. *APU*, pp. 63–82 and *passim*.

4. Jean Wahl, *The Pluralist Philosophies of England & America*, trans. Fred Rothwell (London: Open Court Co., 1925), pp. 62–96.

5. Maitland himself was responsible for translating sections of Otto Von Gierke's *Das Deutsche Genossenscahftsrecht.*

6. In fact, Laski begins the book by using James's definition of America. See Harold J. Laski, *Studies in the Problem of Sovereignty* (New York: Howard Fertig, 1968). For other statements of his indebtedness to James, see *The Foundations of Sovereignty and Other Essays* (New York: Harcourt, Brace, 1921), p. 169, and *The Grammar of Politics* (New Haven, CT: Yale University Press, 1925), p. 261.

7. *Holmes-Laski Letters: The Correspondence of Mr. Justice Holmes and Harold J. Laski, 1916–1935*, vol. 1, ed. Mark De Wolfe Howe (Cambridge, MA: Harvard University Press, 1953), p. 633.

8. Harold J. Laski, *Studies in Law and Politics* (New Haven, CT: Yale University Press, 1932), pp. 244.

9. Laski, *Studies in Law and Politics*, 259.

10. Laski, *The Foundations of Sovereignty*, p. 168.

11. Laski, *The Foundations of Sovereignty*, 87.

12. Laski, *The Foundations of Sovereignty*, 180.

13. Although Laski denies that he, himself, is a "Jamesian." *Holmes-Laski Letters*, pp. 69, 71, 633. In *The Metaphysical Club*, Louis Menand ignores Holmes's dislike of James's philosophy, choosing instead to describe them both as pluralists and pragmatists—a claim that Holmes would likely find outrageous.

14. Figgis's reputation rests almost exclusively on his *Churches in the Modern State* (London: Longmans, 1914).

15. Figgis, *Churches in the Modern State*, 80.

16. G. D. H. Cole, *Guild Socialism Restated* (London: L. Parsons, 1920), pp. 120–24.

17. G. D. H. Cole, *The Social Theory* (London: Methuen and Co., 1920), esp. chapter 4, "Democracy and Representation."

18. Cole, *The Social Theory*, pp. 134–37.

19. Harold J. Laski, *Authority in the Modern State* (New Haven, CT: Yale University Press, 1919).

20. Robert MacIver, *The Web of Government* (New York: Macmillan Company, 1947), p. 56.

21. Harold Laski, *A Grammar of Politics* (London: George Allen and Unwin, Ltd., 1930), pp. 424–30.

22. John Dewey to Horace M. Kallen, March 31, 1915, Horace M. Kallen Collection, American Jewish Archives, Hebrew Union College, Cincinnati, quoted by Menand, p. 400.

23. John Dewey, "Nationalizing Education" (1916), *The Middle Works, 1899–1924*, ed. Jo Ann Boydston (Carbondale: Southern Illinois University Press, 1976–83), vol. 10, p. 205, quoted *ibid.*

24. Cf. John Dewey, *The Public and its Problems* (New York: Henry Holt and Co., 1927).

25. Kung Chuan Hsiao, *Political Pluralism: A Study in Contemporary Political Theory* (New York: Harcourt, Brace & Company, 1927), p. 172.

26. This from Laski in a review of Hsaio's book. "Political Pluralism," *The New Republic* 54, no. 695 (March 28, 1928), p. 197.

27. Hsiao, *Political Pluralism*, p. 149.
28. Hsiao, *Political Pluralism*, pp. 175–208.
29. David B. Truman will declare Hsiao's book to be the very best in the history of political pluralism, a declaration found in *The Governmental Process: Political Interests and Public Opinion* (New York: Alfred A. Knopf, 1951). He does so, in my opinion, for this very reason.
30. Henry Meyer Magid, *English Political Pluralism: The Problem of Freedom and Organization* (New York: Columbia University Press, 1941), p. 65.
31. See Magid, *English Political Pluralism*, p. 43.
32. Magid, *English Political Pluralism*, pp. 3–4.
33. Magid, *English Political Pluralism*, p. 74.
34. Compare the optimism of Magid's conclusion with his intellectual forebears. "Democracy," he writes, "solves the problem of freedom by recognizing and permitting the existence of . . . cultural pluralism, restricting its regulating function solely to those actions of the group which raise communal problems." Magid, *English Political Pluralism*, p. 92.
35. Perhaps the most representative of these books, or at least the most canonical, are David B. Truman's *The Governmental Process: Political Interests and Public Opinion* (New York: Alfred A. Knopf, 1955) and Robert Dahl's *Pluralist Democracy in the United States: Conflict and Consent* (Chicago: Rand McNally & Co., 1967).
36. See, for example, T. Vernor Smith's *The Promise of American Politics* (Chicago: University of Chicago Press, 1936) for an early version of this sentiment, though one that does not claim the mantle of pluralism. Smith saw his political theory as nonpluralist primarily because the pluralism of Smith's time was still partially Jamesian.
37. Samuel Huntington, *The Clash of Civilizations and the Remaking of World Order* (New York: Simon & Schuster, 1998); *Who We Are: The Challenges to America's National Identity* (New York: Simon & Schuster, 2004).
38. William Connolly, "The Challenge to Pluralist Theory," *The Bias of Pluralism*, ed. William Connolly (New York: Atherton Press, 1969).
39. Robert Dahl, *A Preface to Democratic Theory* (Chicago: University of Chicago Press, 1956).
40. Dahl, *The Governmental Process*, pp. 14–23, 33.
41. Kirstie McClure, "On the Subject of Rights: Pluralism, Plurality, and Political Identity," *Dimensions of Radical Democracy: Pluralism, Citizenship, Community*, ed. Chantal Mouffe (New York: Verso, 1992), p. 119.
42. See Dahl, *Dilemmas of Pluralist Democracy: Autonomy vs. Control* (New Haven, CT: Yale University Press, 1982).
43. Henry S. Kariel, *The Decline of American Pluralism* (Stanford, CA: Stanford University Press, 1961), pp. 126–27.
44. C. Wright Mills, *The Power Elite* (Oxford, UK: Oxford University Press, 1956), especially 242–68.
45. Kariel, *The Decline of American Pluralism*, p. 133.
46. W. J. Mackenzie, "Representation in Plural Societies," *Political Studies* 2, no. 1 (Feb. 1954), pp. 54–69.

47. *Responsibility and Judgment*, ed. Jerome Kohn (New York: Shocken Books, 2003), pp. 193–213. James Bohman has excellently characterized Arendt's false dichotomy between the politics of equality and sameness in his essay, "The Moral Costs of Political Pluralism," in *Hannah Arendt: Twenty Years Later*, ed. Larry May and Jerome Kohn (Cambridge, MA: MIT Press, 1996), pp. 53–80.

48. Isaiah Berlin, *Four Essays on Liberty* (New York: Oxford University Press, 1969).

49. Alex Zakaras emphasizes these qualities in his essay "Isaiah Berlin's Cosmopolitan Ethics," *Political Theory* 32, no. 4 (August 2003), pp. 495–518.

50. Isaiah Berlin, *The Roots of Romanticism*, ed. Henry Hardy (Princeton, NJ: Princeton University Press, 1999), 146.

51. See, for example, his essays on Herder and Montesquieu in, respectively, *Vico and Herder: Two Studies in the History of Ideas* (London: Hogarth Press, 1976) and *Against the Current: Essays in the History of Ideas*, ed. Henry Hardy (New York: Viking, 1980).

52. Berlin, *Four Essays*, 132–33.

53. Harold Laski, *Liberty in the Modern State* (New York: Viking Press, 1949), 37.

54. Often, this line of argument extends even to his supporters, who endeavor to place Berlin on firm foundations. See George Crowder, *Liberalism and Value Pluralism* (London: Continuum, 2002), C. B. Macpherson, *Democratic Theory: Essays in Retrieval* (Oxford, UK: Clarendon Press, 1973), and Leo Strauss, *The Rebirth of Classical Political Rationalism: An Introduction to the Thought of Leo Strauss*, ed. Thomas Pangle (Chicago: Chicago University Press, 1989); for defenders who make similar insistences, see John Gray, *Two Faces of Liberalism* (New York: The New Press, 2000), Jonathan Riley, "Interpreting Berlin's Liberalism," *American Political Science Review* 95 (June 2001), and Robert Kocis, *A Critical Appraisal of Sir Isaiah Berlin's Political Philosophy* (Lewiston, NY: The Edward Mellen Press, 1989).

55. For an extended critique of Berlinian negative freedom along these lines, see Thomas L. Dumm, *Michel Foucault and the Politics of Freedom* (Thousand Oaks, CA: Sage Publications, 1996), pp. 47–63.

56. C. B. Macpherson, *Democratic Theory: Essays in Retrieval* (Oxford, UK: Clarendon Press, 1973), p. 186.

57. See, for example, Avigail Eisenberg, *Reconstructing Political Pluralism* (Albany: State University of New York Press, 1995).

# 3

# Sovereignty, Self-Determination, and the Nation

JAMES CLEARLY CRITICIZED HEGEL'S IDEALS of oneness and of systemic absolutism. The Jamesians who follow him, at least at first, were equally clear: The common insistence on the ideal of unified solidarity is the largest threat to the body politic. The alternative modes of being celebrated by James and his followers pose a threat to the consolidation of a politico-philosophical-national culture by their very nature.

In the terms of traditional political theory, James thus stands as a censure to the conception of sovereignty. For the Hobbesian sovereign or the Rousseauian General Will or the Hegelian *Geist* to exist, those who oppose it (or even seek to remain unsubsumed by it) must be either overcome or destroyed. Whether king or people, a sovereign power cannot allow fundamental differences—a house divided against itself can never stand.

But there exists another sense of sovereignty which coincided with James's notion of individualism and self-determination: that of states in an international framework. For while James saw pluralism as recognizing the existence and legitimacy of other people's lives, he equally saw it as recognizing the existence and legitimacy of other cultural lives. Indeed, the very development of his antipathy toward imperialism coincided with his philosophical embrace of pluralism.

## Sovereignty

The problem of sovereignty in its international capacities stands central to the question of nationhood. Long seen as essential to the identity of states, and thus the highest aspiration of nationhood, sovereignty is to states what liberty is to individuals: theoretically, the right to determine one's own actions without interference. Like the politically constituted subject, the ideal state is conceived as autonomous.

Within politics, contemporary sovereignty is thus understood as the ultimate aspiration of a nation, its fundamental completion. Yet sovereignty has never fulfilled this promise; the history of state sovereignty emerges as one of coercion, war, and intervention. If sovereignty were as obvious and as easy as its celebrants claim, its abridgments would be appalling and rare. In reality, states cannot actually be fully sovereign, no matter how strenuously their leaders claim that they are. The first half of this chapter builds on contemporary examinations of sovereignty that identify its exclusions and limitations, arguing that the underlying theoretical construction of sovereignty also fatally undermines its ideals.

Yet the philosophy of sovereignty has a history, having been deployed in ways both salutary and pernicious. The chapter's second half excavates an alternative conception of sovereignty, one that exalts the heterogeneity of nations and states as central to comprehending the significance of a state's self-identity. The United States engaged in its most wide-ranging imperialist expansion ever at the beginning of the twentieth century, increasing its control over distant countries including Hawai'i and the Philippines. An explicit connection emerged contemporaneously between anti-imperialism and the celebration of autonomy—connections most overtly made formal in the thought of William James. Through these correlations, an alternative, pluralist conception of sovereignty emerged, one with the potential to inform our contemporary understandings of international relations.

## Intersections of Sovereignties

Sovereignty as a conceptual basis for national autonomy has emerged during the last four centuries as the dominant theoretical basis for understanding relationships between states. The idea that states have the moral and political right to ultimate self-governance, as developed by Jean Bodin and Thomas Hobbes, is largely taken for granted in the formulation of international policy and state relations. And yet the problems of sovereignty, the theoretical justifications for the unconditional dominance of state-centered absolutism, are increasingly contested, both within academic thought and everyday practices.

The end of the Cold War, the dominance of transnational capital, the explosion of information and communication technologies, and the emergence of international terrorism provide the customary reasons for this contestation. But the inconsistencies of sovereignty far predate these contemporary events. From its intellectual founding, sovereignty has needed to neglect or repress alternative conceptions of authority; the problems of founding a state and the problems of founding an intellectual justification for that state have been intertwined from the beginning.[1]

In attempting to replace the complexities of theological authority and economic feudalism with a specifically political nationalism, the architects of sovereignty constructed a world where only the state could authorize political action and where political identities were reduced to citizenship. Yet in this construction (and in the necessary overthrow of the previous authorities), these theories reconstituted human identity in ways that subverted the goals of sovereignty: In creating political identities that resisted previous powers, political identities that could resist the new governance were created as well.

Hobbes, for example, famously grounded the sovereign's authority in the protection of the individual. The Leviathan protects each person from the "war of all against all" that naturally arises from the essential equality of men. In doing so, Hobbes necessarily privileges the autonomy of the individual as not only the purpose of the state, but also as its cause. His fictional "state of nature" narrative serves to position the state as the necessary counterbalance to the inherent sovereignty of human beings. Without the contractual unification of self-governing humans, their autonomy sabotages itself. To create the sovereignty of the state, Hobbes must produce the sovereign individual. He recognizes that this causes sovereignty to be based on intrinsically unstable support—thus, he indicates the limitation that one is free from one's political obligations when the sovereign threatens one's life.

The sovereignty of the state, therefore, rests on its exact opposite. If individuals are truly sovereign, as Hobbes insists more strongly than anyone before him, then state power is vestigial and parasitic. Thus, the power of the Leviathan must be strengthened in order to simultaneously protect and obliterate this individual sovereignty. But the individual must also acquiesce to this obliteration—the individual who is the implicit reader of Hobbes's text—the individual who will subsequently reason that the state's power is justified.[2]

Positioning this conflict as central to the sovereignty project explains many of the peculiarities that arise in the history of sovereignty. Both Hobbes and Bodin, for example, insisted on the impossibility of sovereign alienation: They both argued that the rights of monarchs cannot be relinquished, circumscribed, or estranged. Yet their very imperativeness points to their apprehension about its possibility. Why bother, one may ask, to insist that the impossible cannot happen? Similarly, as David Campbell contends in his work on Bosnia, the entire premise of Hobbesian order necessarily bases itself on the (putatively) inescapable reality of disorder.[3] The work of subject formation, both that of the individual and of the nation, therefore serves to justify the exclusion, even the violent exclusion, of those who are unable to be integrated into the sovereignty that is presupposed as necessary.[4]

In other words, Bodin and Hobbes constructed a system of interdependence between the autonomy of the subject and the authority of the state. And yet autonomy by its very nature is supposed to be, well, autonomous: absolute, independent, and unconstrained. Interdependent autonomies contradict themselves. Additionally, these mutually iterated sovereignties, that of the subject and that of the state, cannot possibly coexist: as Daniel Warner has noted, the claims of the state upon the individual are limited by no power external to the state.[5] Even a reversal of the Hobbesian relation between state and populace—as in Rousseau's insistence that the people instead of the government are sovereign or Hegel's contention that the state is the concrete manifestation of the will of the people—shows that the sovereignty of the individual cannot coexist with the will of the nation. The hierarchy of freedom and authority that each theorist constructs, for all the differences between them, results in the dissolution of subjectivity into citizen.[6]

Thus, the project of politics becomes the negotiation of these incommensurable yet mutually foundational ideas. "The new modern world of spatially separated sovereigns and subjects having been constituted," as Rob Walker writes, the theoretical project becomes "that of working out how it could be put back together again—how individual and collective, public and private, state sovereignty and public sovereignty, and so on, could be reconciled."[7] Those questions and paradoxes, in short, have underlain the question of sovereignty—and thus of individual subjects, nation-states, and politics generally—throughout modernity.

Other alleged sources of sovereignty are similarly foundationally troubled. The Treaty of Westphalia, often identified by international relations scholars as the emergence of interstate sovereignty, constitutes a turning point in establishing a horizontal space of states as Europe's primary actors. The Westphalian logic underlying the mutuality of state recognition is generally understood as giving nation-states the authority to speak for their resident populations: each government, however constituted, recognizes (or does not recognize) another government as its sovereign equal.

The Peace of Westphalia did not create these relations wholesale, of course.[8] But it shaped the system which had emerged in fits and starts through the seventeenth century into a particularly idealized form which remains with us today. Those who controlled the mechanisms of state formalized and mediated relations of power, which both created an interstate system and reified the legitimation of those individuals as the sole and authentic leaders of "their" territories and peoples, a legitimation that was constituted from without as well as from within.

There are two noteworthy aspects to this process. The first and most obvious is that the sovereignty of states did not immediately become widely accepted upon the signing of the treaty, even in Europe: The Holy Roman Empire prospered until the beginning of the nineteenth century and many cities and fiefdoms in areas such as present-day Italy fiercely resisted statist consolidation.[9] State sovereignty, in other words, did not instantly triumph; the battles between it and other forms of political power both predate and antedate Westphalia.

Most historical accounts of interstate acceptance of sovereignty explain these battles as a delay in intellectual development. F. H. Hinsley, for example, contended that Westphalian conceptions did not immediately become ubiquitous due to people's inability to epistemologically comprehend that the world was "composed of separate political communities."[10] This analysis may seem correct in hindsight, but only if the development of the contemporary interstate system was in fact teleologically inescapable, if our contemporary arrangement of the state system constitutes the absolute and correct answer to the problems of the distribution of political power. But for those for whom authority ought not be reducible to the state, for those whose identities exceed, undercut, or are more complex than that of "citizen," the spatially limited but absolute power of the state was seen as disabling, pernicious, or even sacrilegious. Indeed, for many, it continues to be so.

The second noteworthy aspect of the Westphalian process is that its ideal of sovereignty implicitly depends on that which it denies, akin to the contradictions of Hobbesian sovereignty. International sovereignty, the exclusive and total authority within the borders of the state, cannot truly be exclusive nor total; if the international system endows this authority, then that authority always rests, at least in part, on the recognition of those from outside the state. The very existence and being of a "sovereign entity," then, "presupposes an institutional framework in which it is recognized by others."[11] The goal and design of sovereignty, to be free from dependence on alternative sources of power, is therefore subverted by the recognition required for its constitution.

The idea that such recognition relies at least partially on extrasovereign sources has long been emphasized by opponents or the "realist" approach to international relations, who hope to replace it with approaches emphasizing norms and institutions.[12] But even the vast majority of these theories do not fundamentally critique the dilemmas of a putative sovereignty that relies on institutional frameworks. These authors unproblematically accept sovereignty as the precondition of their theories, and then argue that norms and organizations mitigate the anarchic effects of that sovereignty. States are seen as sovereign entities around which networks of control and recognition are to be built; those networks are not properly seen as constitutive of the very existences and definitions of the sovereign states.

The constituted nature of sovereignty is made more tangible through accounts which describe it as a normalizing development: historically located, partial, and in constant need of reinscription.[13] At their best, such approaches not only emphasize that sovereignty depends upon fictions that must be developed, but also that these fictions must be enforced through bloodshed and cruelty. In addition, the fact that claims to sovereignty are necessarily oriented to external constituencies (such as China decrying the involvement of human rights organizations in its "internal affairs") undermines the very assertion on which they are based, both in audience (to whom is China speaking?) and in intent (why does China feel the need to speak at all?). Such exteriority belies the understanding of sovereignty as intrinsically autonomous.[14] These difficulties are made manifest in the practices of sovereignty, for example the oft-noted incongruity that countries who most insist on the actuality of sovereignty (for example, the United States) tend to repeatedly find vindications for cross-national intervention.

These difficulties, intrinsic to the very concept of sovereignty, have resulted in many international relations specialists throughout the twentieth century calling for the concept's eradication from politics and political science. Numerous writers—Charles Merriman at the turn of the century, Harold Laski and Léon Duguit in the World War I period, and R. M. MacIver and Jacques Maritain at mid-century—argued that the concept of sovereignty lacked legal foundation, historical precedent, philosophical usefulness, or empirical authenticity.[15] All decried sovereignty as a bankrupt concept, used by states as a cover for intervention, as a justification for blindness to human suffering, as an excuse to inflict ruthless cruelties, and should thus be banished from the lexicon of international concerns.

And yet the language of sovereignty continues unabated: it remains perhaps the most used and reused trope in the international vocabulary. What does a government claim if it wishes to turn aside criticism of its human rights record? Sovereignty. What is bolstered by the Law of the Sea? Sovereignty. What does the World Trade Organization protect? Sovereignty. What American resource faces threats via creeping one-worldism? Sovereignty. What is the highest and proper desire of those people whose countries have been invaded? Again, sovereignty.

In other words, completely rejecting the terminology of sovereignty is undoubtedly implausible, though some would still strive to move "beyond sovereignty."[16] For one, it is deeply enough ingrained that its use would be virtually impossible to terminate. But not only does it underlie the linguistic structures and normative assumptions of interstate relations, the term also continues to have useful purposes: serving as a theoretical and utilitarian bulwark, for example, against the excesses of international capital and global homogenization. An idealized national independence also has intense rhetorical and emotional force in the case of those peoples forced to undergo hundreds of years of colonialism under the brutality of Western imperialism.[17] Sovereignty clearly has its uses. And yet the intrinsic contradictions within the very concept make it impossible to use unproblematically.

In recent years, international relations scholars have refigured the sovereignty problematic in new ways. By focusing on the historical developments within sovereignty, they have emphasized how it has replaced the political predicaments that it purports to solve with new ones. For example, the ontological insecurity at the base of the nation-state might be displaced by constructing a threat of the "foreign," as Richard Ashley and David Campbell have argued.[18] Others, such as Rob Walker and Cynthia Enloe, have examined what states do with nonstate actors with negligible access to state decision-making, and how those actors respond.[19] Examining the complicity between authority and global capitalism has been Michael Hardt and Antonio Negri's approach; critiquing the underlying symbolic construction of state legitimacy has been James Der Derian and Michael Shapiro's.[20] Finally, there are those such as Steven Krasner and Cynthia Weber who confront the concept of sovereignty directly, arguing that one can understand it only as an historical "simulation," wherein the false oppositions of "intervention" and "sovereignty" are seemingly adversarial but in fact continuously justify one another, where sovereignty and threats to sovereignty replace and reinforce one another.[21]

All of these approaches recognize that sovereignty is not an essential or natural characteristic of states. Instead, they consider the ways in which states construct themselves in relation to philosophical, linguistic, and historical practices. The variety of practices constitute sovereignty as a crucially multifarious artifact, a part of the international world that always works fragmentarily. The language of closed, clean, and clear political self-determination for states always papers over interconnections, mutual reinforcements, and more often than not the overt denial of others' similar rights. Sovereignty, they show, promises a closure which can never come.

## Jamesian Sovereignty

Rather than further reiterating the ultimate indecipherability of sovereignty, I return to James to investigate a particular historical conception of sovereignty, a way in which it was popularized as an appropriate vehicle for national identity. Before the Cold War's absolute conflation of sovereignty with ideology, before the Germanic conception of a fascist sovereignty as the culmination of a people's solidarity, before the Wilsonian iteration of sovereignty as the automatically liberal/capitalist goal for peoples not yet competent to achieve that aim, before all of these was an understanding of sovereignty that both helped form its contemporary conceptions and provided a convincing alternative to them.

For William James, the right of people to determine their own destiny was morally crucial. He asserted an emphatic conception of sovereignty. It was central to the rights of states, the substance of international relations, and the ethical practice of governance; James notably did not have the latter-day suspicion of the goals of the nation-state. National independence stood as the highest good to which a people could aspire, and its achievement was to be celebrated.

But intrinsic to Jamesian sovereignty was a radically pluralistic streak, one that went missing just two decades later in the Wilsonian ideology of self-determination that ostensibly resembled James's. James held sacrosanct the ability to create one's own destiny, but it remained a power that was informed by and dependent on others. States, like individuals, could never truly exist on their own, he argued; it is only through difference and contestation that either can truly reach its full potential and achieve the richness of a well-lived life. This pluralist tychism set James's philosophy and international politics apart—both from his contemporaries and from those who came after him.

It is of primary importance to distinguish Jamesian pluralism from the later philosophic trajectory of the concept of "political pluralism" discussed in the last chapter. The better-known pluralism that emerged during the course of the twentieth century (such as that of Robert Dahl), where the state functions as a formal but normatively empty structure through which various interest groups contest one another, bears virtually no resemblance to James's celebration of pluralist difference.[22]

The term *pluralism* is even occasionally used within the field of international relations as a replacement for *liberalism* or *idealism*; obviously this usage, too, descends from its original meaning, but also reinforces the term's alienation from James's usage. For James, pluralism and difference were an aspiration; without oppositional ways of making sense of the world, he argued, life can have no significance. For latter-day pluralists, on the other hand, pluralism simply describes a messy fact of modern-day life, requiring states and systems to negotiate those unpleasant dissimilarities of political coalitions and interest groups. Such a conception relies on a severe impoverishment of plurality, positioning difference as exclusively organizational, that is, as consisting of "autonomous organizations within the domain of a state."[23]

Just as in philosophy, James saw in the world a demand toward sameness and unity, a presumption that leading others to the correct path is the point of systems, be they intellectual or political. But the different experiences of all people (and peoples) show these projects' inherent unsuitability and undesirability. If a state has a monopoly on a way of life, it could be justified in violently forcing another people to live its way; if not, perhaps it should learn from others and define itself in opposition to them rather than overcoming them. That other people could live in ways that are unusual to us, even alien to our standards, gives meaning to our own ways of life, according to James.

James told a personal parable to drive the point home in a public lecture. Once, when on train traversing the North Carolinian wilderness, he informed his listeners, he looked out of the window and saw a scarified land: a clearing where trees had been blasted from the ground, a cabin rough-hewn and out of plumb, and a serpentine fence going nowhere and offering protection from nothing. Squalor in the midst of a sylvan idyll, this clearing affronted James's sensibilities, at least at first: it showed the very baseness of man's development and his generalized disregard for the beauty of nature. But upon further reflection, and upon discussing the ethos of progress that informed the denizens of nearby comparable homes, James realized something far different was at work.

It was not that the residents did not see this house as an affront to nature. Like James's, their understanding was that such a clearing was antithetical to the natural order. But unlike him, they saw such an affront as a victory: the working man's ability to transform the disordered wilderness into civilization. The clearing, James pointed out to his audience, "which was to me a mere ugly picture on the retina, was to them a symbol redolent with moral memories and sang a very paean of duty, struggle, and success."[24] James recognized that his own limitations blinded him to the "significance" of such constructions; his cultural and social position discouraged an ability to understand the legitimacy of others' worlds.

This is not merely an example of the tolerating liberalism of the late twentieth century, where one is meant to endure the dissimilarities of others. James did not simply allow others to destroy "their" woods while leaving his in peace (or, worse, attempt to convince these others that their figurative struggle against nature was wrong, or misguided, or contraposed to historical reality). Instead, his is a constitutive, active, embrace of the *need* for difference: James considered himself transformed, elevated, and educated by this incidental encounter with a way of life dissimilar from his own. Without this realization, James recounted, he would have continued his life intellectually impoverished, blind to the legitimacy of the rural landworkers' views.

## Sovereignty, Dependence, and Difference

So what, exactly, is the relationship between a Jamesian radical pluralism and the aforementioned sovereignty problematic? Historically, James became well known to the American people not just for his construction of pragmatism but for his public pronouncements—letters, essays, speeches—against American imperialism. A second aspect emerges from the degree to which internationalization and globalization were central questions in his time; when James began to be interested in international affairs, the international economy was profoundly integrated, by some measurements even more than it is presently.[25] Third, these two interests emerged in tandem. In the last decade of his life he emerged both as a publicly renowned pacifist/anti-imperialist and as a pluralist. As James became increasingly interested in pluralism, he was also positioning himself against his former student, Theodore Roosevelt, in a series of letters published in national newspapers. In these letters, James defended the right to dissent publicly, the right to self-governance, and ultimately, the right for other nations to exist on terms the United States might never understand.[26]

Though most philosophical biographies overlook this aspect of his thought, it was well known at the time and contributed to the popular reception given both pragmatism and pluralism. Publicly, James most closely identified with his criticism of McKinleyite imperialism. The capriciousness of the Spanish-American War, the annexation of the Philippines, and the United States's involvement in the overthrow of the Hawaiian monarchy all drove James to speak out against the imposition of American power on other countries.[27]

His public stance was slow to make itself known. Privately, in personal letters to his friends and colleagues, James criticized the "madness" of the U.S. Congress as early as the 1898 sinking of the *Maine*; even in the "perfectly honest humanitarianism" of the American emotional response, he already saw the seeds of the imperialism to come.[28] As the crisis with Spain escalated, James became fascinated with the ways in which a political administration interested in expansion stimulated and exercised the psychology of crowds, and he began to suspect the ideological underpinnings of the U.S. government's creation of excitement and heroism that enabled it to act in violent and warlike ways.

But not until the turn of the century did James publicly (and vociferously) criticize the McKinley administration's peremptory colonization of the Philippines. In a series of letters to influential newspapers, James decried American involvements abroad, identifying as "hegelian" the misguided idea that all countries should share the same goals and aims, and that the United States could thus show the way to other states. The essential multiplicity of humanity, he argued, made the domination of others fundamentally immoral;

the United States, therefore, did not and could not have the right to control the destinies of other countries. James's public pronouncements continued likewise until his death in 1910. He persistently expressed his outrage at imperialism in all its forms and repeatedly criticized it despite his failing health.

James's arguments stood in clear contrast to the Mugwumpery of the era's other prominent anti-imperialists. Even beyond the actual Mugwumps, who regarded the end of American isolationism as imperialism's worst effect, other predominant anti-imperialists gave dubious reasons for their opposition. E. L. Godkin, editor of *The Nation* and *The New York Evening Post*, was famous for his antipathy to American imperialism, but he based his opposition on a proudly racist conception of how colonialism debased the ideals of Americanism, and how close contact with "alien, inferior, and mongrel races" would infect Americans.[29] Edward Atkinson's popular opposition to American involvement in the Philippines came largely from his conviction that American boys would return from abroad infected with "venereal disease"; sex and sickness, naturally alien to America, throve in the tropics.[30] Andrew Carnegie, the wealthiest of the anti-imperialists, fulminated publicly about the cost of imperialism, the damage to American "moral fiber," and the loss of international respect.[31] All three of these public figures shared, in their opposition to the expansionist foreign policy of the McKinley and Roosevelt administrations, a concern not for the non-Americans being invaded and killed, but for the damaging effects of colonialism and imperialism on the citizens of the United States.

James, on the contrary, argued against expansionism on the grounds that the American presumptions that underlay imperialism were neither necessary nor beneficial to the colonized. The United States, he contended, could not understand other cultures and thus had no right attempting to shape or control them. The sovereignty of other nations, for James, was not precisely identical to the individual pluralism he professed, but the same mistrust of absolutism and unity undergirded both ideals. The internal truth of different individuals and the internal truth of different cultures, he believed, were linked; one cannot accept the empirical authenticity of the first without also recognizing the latter. For James, the admission of these truths necessitated respect for these others, be they people or countries. One country imposing its system of government on another is injurious—not merely for the nation imposed upon, but for the ethical constitution of the empire-minded country. The latter needs to begin learning from alterity rather than merely conquering it.

James's opposition to the United States's annexing the Philippines, which he extensively criticized for a decade, had more to do with the liberties and rights of the Filipinos than with that annexation's effects on Americans. Not, as in Mugwumpery, because the United States was drawn down to the inferior level of the rest of the world's peoples but, in James's view, because those peoples were not inferior. In this, James resisted both the imperialist's language of the necessity to improve the Filipino character (in fact, he pointed out, the United States was massacring Filipinos, which hardly improved anyone's character) and the anti-imperialists' nativist focus.[32] In one series of arguments against American intervention in the Philippines, James inveighed against the emotional and intellectual distance that the Americans perpetuate between themselves and the Filipinos. The United States, he said, tries to organize the world according to its own principles and conceptions, and thus ignores the possibility that the objects of American intrigues "could have any feeling or insides of their own whatever that might possibly need to be considered in our arrangements."[33] He argued that it was impossible for U.S. politicians to regulate the "souls" of the Filipinos, since these politicians could not even understand other Americans' souls.[34]

In 1904, James continued to argue that American interventionism in the Philippines resulted from an inability to let other countries constitute their own national identities. "Let the Filipino leaders try their own system," he argued, "no people learns to live except by trying."[35] And American concerns, though concealed in a cloak of morality, could not adequately justify the oppression of others, even if those others did not correspond to particularly American conceptions of the moral:

> if they fail to be good exactly according to our notions, is not the world full even now of other people of whom the same can be said, and for whose bad conduct towards one another we agree that it would be folly to make ourselves responsible?"[36]

James overtly drew parallels between the autonomy of individuals, which he positioned as universally accepted by his audience, and that of nations, which deserve the same liberties, even if they fail to live up to what American eyes perceive as their responsibilities.

President Taft, he argued, aspired to keep the Filipinos in check so long as their goals differed from those of the United States—that is to say, forever. "We are to 'give' the Philipino true liberty instead of the false liberty he aspires to; we are to reveal his better self to him, to be his savior against his own weakness."[37] America's pose of supremacy, which justified its continued domination over the Philippines, emerged not from moral superiority but from the conflation of military control and cultural difference. Like the United States's historical relation to its own indigenes, recognized differences between the dominant culture and the other were translated not as distinction but as inferiority.[38] (James, however, would not have drawn this parallel: he remained scandalously silent on the ongoing destruction of American Indians and native cultures.) Thus the United States, James stated, is "openly engaged in crushing out the sacredest thing in this great human world—the attempt of a people long enslaved to attain to the possession of itself, to organize its laws and government, to be free to follow its internal destinies according to its own ideals."[39]

Philosophically, James made possible a hermeneutics of cultures; politically, he demanded acknowledgment of the right of other peoples to determine the terms for their own existence. His conception of sovereignty related closely to nationalism (there is no hint in his writings, for example, that the Philippines are not naturally unitary—he groups all Filipinos into a monolithic, undifferentiated mass whose overall approach is presumed to be unproblematically collective), but he changed the underlying language of legitimacy of nationhood. No longer should the United States, or even the West, define which countries are worthy of sovereignty and which need to be pushed to that point of readiness; it should be those countries themselves. Such "international comparisons," James argues,

> are a great waste of time—at any rate, international judgments and the passing of sentences are. Every nation has ideals and difficulties and sentiments which are an impenetrable secret to one not of the blood. Let them alone. . . .[40]

Sovereignty, in this conception, is self-legitimating, accruing naturally to a people. The distance between nations makes it consistently unjust for the people of one country to claim to know what is better for a people than the people themselves. Indeed, it makes it impossible for outsiders to truly lead another nation. That the United States imposes its own version of control over the Filipinos constitutes a fundamental affront to this version of sovereignty.

The same insult would reemerge half a century later, when the United States "relinquishes sovereignty" over the Philippines in 1946. As Roxanne Lynn Doty points out, the term "sovereignty" in this case continued to operate at a purely symbolic level. What, for example, is one to make of the United States continuing to determine policy for the Philippines in the areas of trade (occasionally in direct violation of the Philippine Constitution) and in the regulation of arms purchases? What, Doty asks, is the meaning of the term "sovereignty" when all its "empirical referents" appear to be "missing"?[41] The version of sovereignty prevalent in the United States at the time (and, one could argue, presently) encourages such actions; a Jamesian interpretation would overtly proscribe them.

## Pluralism and Substance

James's respectful pluralism extended beyond his interest in international state affairs, of course. James saw the threats of centralization of the modern world in many forms and in many locations, all leading toward the "Hegelian" demand that all people behave, talk, and think in one allegedly correct way; James's concerns strongly resemble to those which underlie much contemporary opposition to market globalism.[42] James opposed this homogenization, celebrating those people who were overtly unlike him, for it was they who could teach and change him: people who loved war, people who hated nature, people who believed in the afterlife, people who had new ideas of medicine, and Cubans, Hawaiians, and Filipinos.

James's international pluralism is not Wilson's later liberalism. Where Wilson endeavored to give other countries sovereignty, it was a sovereignty along the lines *he* envisioned, a specifically pro-American, free-market, ersatz-Caucasian sovereignty.[43] Those countries failing to meet Wilson's standards of authenticity, such as Mexico or the newly formed Soviet Union, faced unwanted military interventions. An autonomy formed and limited by the economic and political desires of the United States is no autonomy at all. James's radical pluralism, conversely, encouraged the independence of those peoples who specifically differed from American values: those were the countries who most deserved to make their own way in the world. Attempting to mold those countries into pale replicas of the United States was not only the height of arrogance, but denying their continued practical experimentation would impoverish the entire world.

Now, one hundred years after James formulated his version of international pluralism, perhaps we live in a post-imperialist environment, where each set of peoples is indeed free to select the kind of government they most desire, both in form and content. Recent international events, at least since the turn of the millennium, suggest, however, this is not the case. Democratic governments seem less important to the United States than do sympathetic ones; the more powerful interests in the global financial and political systems often intervene in others' affairs, using methods military and economic. That all countries, peoples, and individuals should want to live in the same way, with the same values and the same conceptions of rights, seems to underlay the assumptions of most politicians, tacticians, and others who create and enforce the central issues in relations between countries and cultures.

Even if universal suffrage, sovereignty, and self-determination were the contemporary norm, aspects of Jamesian pluralism could still inform other aspects of international politics. For example, the narrow focus on democratically representative elections currently celebrated by much international foreign policy often serves to legitimize governments at the expense of human rights, minority rights, and civil liberty. What fundamental improvement arises from a popularly elected tyrant immediately suppressing dissent and quashing opposing viewpoints? James demonstrates that instruments of dissent, such as a free press and private associations, have as much civil import as majoritarian rule, if not more. James reminds us that forms of opposition are important in their own right, that the ultimate goal of societies and governments should not be stability but rather the opportunity to express disagreement.

Even further, James explains that opposition allows us to discover those things that are most important to us. He thus creates a different way to think about sovereignty: not as an interstate system of recognition, but as the countenance of alterity that makes identity meaningful. To endorse the sovereignty of others—be they states or individuals—can be as much about challenging ourselves as about demanding recognition. Jamesian pluralism, as an ethical and philosophical system, encourages engagement with the world based on terms we do not ourselves control.

## Notes

1. For many years, in fact for much of the history of political philosophy, the problem of founding has continued as a conundrum for philosophers reaching from Hobbes to Rousseau to Arendt to Rawls to Derrida. See Bonnie Honig, *Political Theory and the Displacement of Politics* (Ithaca, NY: Cornell University Press, 1993).

2. Richard Ashley emphasizes the degree to which it is the rationality of the individual which sets him up as "the modern *sovereign*." See his "Border Lines: Man, Post-Structuralism, and War" in *International/Intertextual Relations*, ed. James Der Derian and Michael Shapiro (New York: Lexington Books, 1989), p. 265.

3. David Campbell, *National Deconstruction: Violence, Identity, and Justice in Bosnia* (Minneapolis: University of Minnesota Press, 1998).

4. Indeed, most of Hobbes's "laws of nature" are based on the social relationships between people. See Sheldon Wolin, *Politics and Vision: Continuity and Innovation in Western Political Thought* (Boston: Little, Brown, 1960).

5. Daniel Warner, "Searching for Responsibility/Community in International Relations," in *Moral Spaces: Rethinking Ethics and World Politics*, ed. David Campbell and Michael Shapiro (Minneapolis: University of Minnesota Press, 1999), 9.

6. Cf. Steven Johnston, *Encountering Tragedy: Rousseau and the Project of Democratic Order* (Ithaca, NY: Cornell University Press, 1999), esp. pp. 75–89.

7. R. B. J. Walker, "Forward," in *Sovereignty and Subjectivity*, ed. Jenny Edkins, Nalani Persram, and Véronique Pin-Fat (Boulder, CO: Lynne Rienner, 1999), p. x.

8. Nor, as Jens Bartleson reminds us, is the concept of the "international" reducible to the advent of the modern state. On the other hand, the two are logically linked, made possible through both shared historical and political developments. See *A Genealogy of Sovereignty* (Cambridge, UK: Cambridge University Press, 1995), p. 209.

9. Alexander B. Murphy provides a nuanced historical reading of these periods in his essay, "The Sovereign State System as Political-Territorial Ideal: Historical and

Contemporary Considerations," in *State Sovereignty as Social Construct*, ed. Thomas J. Biersteker and Cynthia Weber (Cambridge, UK: Cambridge University Press, 1996), pp. 81–120.

10. F. H. Hinsley, *Sovereignty*, 2nd ed., (Cambridge, UK: Cambridge University Press, 1986), p. 159.

11. Alexander Wendt and Daniel Friedheim, "Hierarchy under Anarchy: Informal Empire and the East German State," in *State Sovereignty as Social Construct*, pp. 240–77, esp. 247.

12. See, for a few samples of this approach, James N. Rosenau, *The Study of Global Interdependence: Essays on the Transnationalism of World Affairs* (New York: Nichols, 1980); John A. Vasquez, *The Power of Power Politics: A Critique* (New Brunswick, NJ: Rutgers University Press, 1983); Robert O. Keohane, *After Hegemony: Cooperation and Discord in the World Political Economy* (Princeton, NJ: Princeton University Press, 1984) and, coedited with Joseph Nye, *Transnational Relations and World Politics* (Cambridge, MA: Harvard University Press, 1972); or, more recently, Ernst B. Haas, *Nationalism, Liberalism, and Progress*, vols. 1 and 2 (Ithaca, NY: Cornell University Press 1997, 2000).

13. Cynthia Weber, for example, engages in an extensive and invaluable historiography of ways that "practices of sovereignty" are used to undergird the legitimacy of the state, in *Simulating Sovereignty: Intervention, the State, and Symbolic Exchange* (Cambridge, UK: Cambridge University Press, 1995).

14. For further reflections on this paradox, see Richard K. Ashley and R. B. J. Walker, "Reading Dissidence/Writing the Discipline: Crisis and the Question of Sovereignty in International Studies," *International Studies Quarterly* 34, no. 3, pp. 367–416.

15. Charles E. Merriman, *Studies in the Problem of Sovereignty Since Rousseau* (New York: Columbia University Press, 1990); Harold J. Laski, *The Foundations of Sovereignty and Other Essays* (New York: Harcourt, Brace, 1921) and *Studies in the Problem of Sovereignty* (New York: Howard Fertig, 1968); Léon Duguit, *Law in The Modern State* (New York: Viking Press, 1919); Robert MacIver, *The Web of Government* (New York: MacMillan Company, 1947); Jacques Maritain, *Man and the State* (Chicago: University of Chicago Press, 1957).

16. Maryann K. Cusimano, *Beyond Sovereignty: Issues for a Global Agenda* (New York: Bedford, 2000).

17. Many of these issues are raised in the excellent essays collected by Mark Denham and Mark Owen Lombardi in *Perspectives on Third-World Sovereignty: The Postmodern Paradox* (London: MacMillan Press Ltd., 1996).

18. Richard Ashley, "Untying the Sovereign State: A Double Reading of the Anarchy Problematique," *Millennium* 17 (1988), pp. 227–63; David Campbell, *Writing Security: United States Foreign Policy and the Politics of Identity* (Minneapolis: University of Minnesota Press, 1992).

19. R. B. J. Walker, *One World, Many Worlds: Struggles for a Just World Peace* (Boulder, CO: Lynne Reiner, 1988); Cynthia Enloe, *Bananas, Beaches and Bases: Making Feminist Sense of World Politics* (Berkeley: University of California Press, 2001).

20. Michael Hardt and Antonio Negri, *Empire* (Cambridge, MA: Harvard University Press, 2000), also *Multitude: War and Democracy in the Age of Empire* (London;

Penguin, 2004); James Der Derian, *On Diplomacy: A Genealogy of Western Estrangement* (New York: Basil Blackwell, 1987); Michael J. Shapiro, *Violent Cartographies: Mapping Cultures of War* (Minneapolis: University of Minnesota Press, 1997).

21. Stephen D. Krasner, *Sovereignty: Organized Hypocrisy* (Princeton, NJ: Princeton University Press, 2001); Weber, *Simulating Sovereignty*.

22. Robert Dahl, *Pluralistic Democracy in the United States* (Chicago: Rand McNally & Co, 1967) and *Dilemmas of Pluralist Democracy: Autonomy vs. Control* (New Haven, CT: Yale University Press, 1982).

23. Dahl, *Dilemmas of Pluralist Democracy*, p. 5.

24. "On a Certain Blindness in Human Beings," *Talks to Teachers on Psychology and to Students on Some of Life's Ideals* (New York: Norton, 1958), pp. 133–34. Two noteworthy commentators have taken this story of James's very seriously and argued that it plays a central role in James's political thought; I am indebted to both George Cotkin's *William James, Public Philosopher* (Urbana: University of Illinois Press, 1989) and Joshua L. Miller's *Democratic Temperament: The Legacy of William James* (Lawrence: University Press of Kansas, 1997).

25. Robert Wade, "Globalization and its Limits: Reports of the Death of the International Economy are Grossly Exaggerated," in *National Diversity and Global Capitalism*, ed. Suzanne Berger and Ronald Dore (Ithaca, NY: Cornell University Press, 1996), pp. 73–74.

26. Miller's *Democratic Temperament* convincingly examines this aspect of James's public persona.

27. Two recent authors of note who have helped to rectify this situation are Cotkin, *William James* (see pp. 123–51) and the literary critic Frank Lentricchia "The Return of William James," *Cultural Critique*, no. 4 (Fall 1986), pp. 5–31.

28. See Cotkin, *William James*, pp. 132–33.

29. In *The Nation* (January 13, 1898), 23, quoted in Robert Beisner, *Twelve against Empire: The Anti-Imperialists 1898–1900* (New York: McGraw-Hill, 1968), p. 76.

30. Edward Atkinson to William McKinley, January 26, 1899. Cited in Beisner, *Twelve against Empire*, pp. 97–98.

31. Beisner, *Twelve against Empire*, p. 174.

32. However, James had played a considerable part in building the rhetoric of "American manliness" that was used as a pretext in both the Spanish-American War and the Philippines. See Kim Townsend's *Manhood at Harvard: William James and Others* (New York: W. W. Norton, 1996) and Roxanne Lynn Doty, *Imperial Encounters* (Minneapolis: University of Minnesota Press, 1996), pp. 30–42.

33. "The Philippine Question," in *Essays, Comments, and Reviews* (Cambridge, MA: Harvard University Press, 1987), p. 160.

34. "The Philippines Again," in *Essays, Comments, and Reviews* (Cambridge, MA: Harvard University Press, 1987), 161; see also Cotkin, *William James*, pp. 138–39.

35. "Secretary Taft a Biased Judge," in *Essays, Comments, and Reviews* (Cambridge, MA: Harvard University Press, 1987), p. 179.

36. "Secretary Taft a Biased Judge," pp. 179–80.

37. "Secretary Taft a Biased Judge," p. 178.

38. This being the central thesis of Tzvetan Todorov in *The Conquest of America: The Question of the Other*, trans. Richard Howard (New York: HarperCollins, 1984).

39. "The Philippine Tangle," *Essays, Comments, and Reviews*, p. 156.

40. William James to Mrs. Henry Whitman, October 5, 1999, *Letters of William James*, ed. Henry James (Boston: Atlantic Monthly Press, 1920.) Quoted in Joshua Miller, *The Democratic Temperament*, p. 58.

41. Doty, *Imperial Encounters*, p. 94.

42. E.g., Benjamin R. Barber's *Jihad vs. McWorld* (New York: Times Books, 1995).

43. Though many have commented on Wilson's "diplomacy of idealism," the book which best captures this central ambiguity in Wilson's international affairs is William Appleman Williams, *The Tragedy of American Diplomacy* (New York: Dell, 1962), esp. pp. 52–83.

# 4

# *La Philosophie Américaine*: James, Bergson, and Reverberations of Intercontinental Pluralism

WHO OWNS ANTI-FOUNDATIONALISM? Arguments that truths arise from contextual and plural sources, as well as studies of the social and intellectual environments through which these truth claims arose, have gained surprising attention in the past decade. Not because they are new, necessarily; debates between the Sophists and the Platonists point to similar epistemological fisticuffs. Rather, the decline of Marxism as an institutionalized, statist doctrine underpinning a quasi-expansionist Soviet Union, combined with a marked distrust for universalist, one-size-fits-all mechanistic determinism, has created an opening for more esoteric and pluralistic understandings of political, cultural, and social events.

The accepted narrative explaining these recent years has been relatively and deceptively simple: in the late 1970s, a number of American academics began reading European authors, generally known as *postmodernists* or *poststructuralists*. Convinced by (or seduced by, depending on the political proclivities of the narrator) the arguments of theorists such as Foucault, Derrida, Lyotard, Deleuze, and Latour and their progenitors Heidegger, Merleau-Ponty, and Adorno, scholars replicated their anti-foundationalism, their critical approaches, and their opaque writing style. For those critics who tell this story most often, these tendencies have led to a slippery aestheticization of philosophy, a propensity for jargon which obscures any real argument, and a betrayal of the truth. Defenders, in their turn, show the political potentialities, the intellectual challenge, and the continuing explanatory power of such analyses.[1]

This chapter does not participate in this debate. Instead, I want to challenge its underlying presumption that a European-invading philosophy displaced the pragmatic truth-telling of the Anglo-American world. This insistence on the radical disconnection between English-language and Continental European theory both profoundly misrepresents the foundations of American intellectual history and willfully ignores the cross-currents of philosophical thought predating the advent of postmodernism.

### Across the Great Divide

William James and Henri Bergson embodied this philosophical approach at the beginning of the twentieth century. One American, one French, they were both friends and competitors. Each was the best-known philosophical intellect of his time and place, each transcended the narrows of academia to hold a place in the popular imagination, and each was an unavoidable influence on subsequent minds. Most importantly, each viewed the other as a colleague and an influence, a relationship which remains mostly unexamined today.

Within the United States, James is known as the exemplary American philosopher: He created or at least popularized pragmatism, the philosophy of everyday experience, and he embodied the plainspoken and straightforward style of the Harvard man. He brought philosophy into its own, freeing it from the excessive abstractions of its history, and built a new, streamlined mode of thought which could serve as the foundation of a truly American approach. James, in other words, stands as the rebuttal to European ownership of philosophical inquiry.

But this simplistic story ignores at least three vital truths (as well as disregarding the complexities of pragmatism). First, William James was known and respected far beyond the borders of the United States. Because today's scholars rarely discuss his fame, the implications and effects of his popularity in Europe and beyond are too often discounted or slighted. Thus, the influences and consequences of his thought abroad—the Jamesian reverberations in the philosophy and art of other languages and countries—are lost. Second, James's reputation during his lifetime rested upon far more than his pragmatism: his empiricism, his psychology, and his pluralism held wide recognition. James became solely identified with pragmatism only as his contributions to intellectual history were reduced to their most simplistic levels. Third, James saw himself as part of an international community of philosophers. Certainly he rejected certain European theoretical tendencies, most notably Hegel's, but he drew upon and even promoted other philosophers doing the same. James's personal and intellectual relationship with the French philosopher Henri Bergson epitomizes these engagements, for Bergson both inspired James's pluralism and was himself, in turn, profoundly influenced by James.

My point here is neither to prove that James owed his conceptualization of pluralism to Bergson (which he often modestly claimed) nor to contend that Bergson was ultimately a Jamesian (which he originally denied, but which others asserted). Such an approach too readily becomes a contest over who influenced whom, a discussion of intellectual commodity ownership and usufruct. Instead, I suggest that James's intellectual development arose from a confluence of plural worlds, an imbrication of thought and trajectories that created a rich network of borrowing, inspiration, and creation. In other words, James's thought, while indisputably his own, is itself thoroughly pluralistic, thus inviting investigations of effects and emanations in unexpected and surprising places.

Demonstrating these relationships highlights the groundless superficiality of dividing the past century of theoretical thought into Continental and Anglo-American philosophy. The simplification of these traditions into two warring camps is an ideological move of condensation and simplification, one that fails to represent the true complexity of their intellectual history.[2] Instead, the effects and echoes of Jamesian pluralism—both within his time and through the subsequent international influence of his work—demonstrate a more complex and accurate relationship between influence and thought, reading and writing, originality and debt.

## Bergson

For the last seven years of his life, from 1903 onward (and coinciding with the development and explanation of his pluralism) James praised Henri Bergson publically, in personal letters, and in conversations with friends and philosophers, referring extensively to Bergson's thought as answering a number of philosophy's central questions. James encouraged translation of Bergson's work, wrote to him eagerly, and dedicated the pivotal chapter in *A Pluralistic Universe* to his thought. Bergson, in turn, repeatedly invited James to Europe through the duration of their correspondence and wrote the introduction to the French translation of *Pragmatism*. Neither man wholeheartedly embraced the other's positions, but each held up the other's work as exemplary investigations of the most interesting philosophical questions and readily admitted to being inspired and led by those advances.

As the nineteenth century became the twentieth, the political and intellectual spaces that Bergson and James inhabited were increasingly concerned with the centralization and unification of power and knowledge. Both men entered into a philosophical tradition dominated by Hegelian absolutism, teleology, and unity, and both found such an approach wrongheaded. James and Bergson also argued that traditional conceptualizations of the quandaries of the world had arisen less from the world than from the limitations of our conceptions of intellect. Foremost, each considered the world irreducible to the conventional understandings that logic required: that, in Bergson's words, while "our intelligence loves simplicity," the universe dispenses an infinitely complex and copious range of things, motions, beings, and states.[3]

Understanding their relationship requires at least a schematic comprehension of certain aspects of Bergson's thought. The affinities between the two authors are clear even in a sketch. For example, Bergson's radical post-Darwinian understanding of evolution dovetails closely with James's anti-teleology. In *Creative Evolution*, published in 1907 and translated into English (with James's help) in 1911, Bergson challenged not only the idea of evolution as a steady, upward process, but also the philosophical conceptions of time as knowable and knowledge as primary. For Bergson, evolution occurs not as a problem to be solved, as with Darwin, but as a creative interaction of species with environments. Matter, or creatures, generate their environs as much as they are generated by them; the energy by which both individuals and species interact leads to profound and profligate divergences.

For Bergson, the result of these innumerable evolutionary divergences is the harmony of the present world, but he used *harmony* with many reservations.

> This harmony is far from being as perfect as it has claimed to be. It admits of much discord, because each species, each individual even, retains only a certain impetus from the universal vital impulsion and tends to use this energy in its own interest. . . . Harmony, or rather "complementarity," is revealed only in the mass, in tendencies rather than states.[4]

Like James's ideas of the multiverse, Bergson based the existing world on the diversity, even "discord," of individualism, ultimately positing individual multiplicity as the basis for the apparent harmonies of the world.

Bergson and James's fierce reciprocal admiration was no accident: their approaches, while obviously not identical, related closely, shared many common concerns, and doubtlessly shaped one another. Comparing James's pluralism with two of the most important themes in Bergson's writing demonstrates a variety of important linkages. The first, the importance of time (as experienced in *duration*), is widely recognized as Bergson's greatest insight. The second, the multiplicity of being (as experienced in *memory*), while linked to the first, has received comparatively less attention, both in Bergson's day and in present reimaginings of his writings. Through these two ideas, Bergson's efforts to explain experience ultimately rested upon intrinsically multiplicitous foundations.

Duration (*durée*), the philosophical concept most connected with Bergson, is the "unbounded flux" of time that "gnaws into the future and which swells as it advances."[5] It is through duration that all matter exists, and through duration comes the ceaseless growth, decay, and life of the world. Duration is not a succession of moments, as is popularly believed. Rather, it is the combination of time and motion that encompasses all existence.

Zeno's arrow, which paradoxically never reaches its target, serves as an ideal foil for duration. The paradox arises, Bergson explained, only when we erroneously conceive of the arrow as fixed and rigid at a certain point. But the arrow does not stop, never rests at a station; "the arrow never *is* in any point of its course."[6] Instead, the arrow exists in continuity, through space and time. It, simply, moves. "The absurdity vanishes," Bergson stated, "as soon as we adopt by thought the continuity of the real movement," that is, when duration—not stasis—is considered as real.[7]

Bergson argued that other kinds of duration, other patterns and flows of time, exist alongside our own, generally not comprehended due to our own lived nature. Indeed, our usual patterns of thought, what Bergson called "intellectualism," disregard duration, and thus reify the matter existing within it. We therefore wrongly think of things as static and absolute. The paradox emerges when Zeno philosophizes the arrow, not when one is actually shot. Fixity is merely an internal mode of thought, not a fact about the outside world. Thus, we can think (or, more precisely, "intuit") through and within duration by recognizing the tensions and intensities of external forces.[8]

This is not just an empiricism of lived time, but a mulitiplicity of empiricisms. Bergson considered conceiving time as intrinsically fragmentary as much a mistake as it is to ignore it overall. Duration is complete, though not totalized; it is a becoming-process, not a point of change. As such, duration *multiplies itself*. Gilles Deleuze, in his book on Bergson, explained that

> duration divides up and does so constantly: That is why it is a *multiplicity*. But it does not divide up without changing in kind . . . : That is why it is a nonnumerical multiplicty, where we can speak of "indivisibles" at each stage of the division.[9]

Bergson, always aiming to escape theoretical dualism, argued that duration is both singular and multiple. Duration for Bergson is "a virtual multiplicity, a *singular* reservoir of potential times," says Timothy Murphy, "but this does not mean that time is not also, in actualisation, irreducibly *multiple*."[10]

As such, time is almost impossible to think through. When time is discussed, it is always spatialized, Bergson pointed out. Language, deliberately philosophical or not, remains enmeshed with solids and matter. Words are more about things than they can be about time, unless they are used with the utmost care. Language, like all forms of symbolic representations, serves to isolate, stabilize, and fix, all of which disable an understanding of duration. Whereas science must work within moments and representations, "the principle justification of metaphysics is a break with symbols."[11] Philosophy, in other words, gets bogged down in representative emblems, when it should attend to motion, action, and time.

Bergson's other important pluralism arose from his conception of memory. *Mémoire* serves as the mechanism through which time and selves interact. Though less remarked upon than duration, this concept holds no less centrality within Bergson's thought. The self, like time, is both unitary and multiplicitous, primarily because the self is made up not of physical substance, but of experience and memory.

"The past is never dead," wrote Faulkner. "It's not even past."[12] This Bergsonian phrasing nicely sums up the constant presence of memory in identity. The present, for Bergson, is active yet meaningless, while the past, though inactive and unchangeable, ultimately *is*. The past exists eternally, as the constant basis for meaning and understanding and selfhood, whereas the present merely is where we make sense of what has come before: "We do not move from the present to the past, from perception to recollection, but from the past to the present, from recollection to perception."[13] All that we have gone through now makes up who we are: no self exists outside of the continuity of experience.

However, memory, while continuous, must also be partial and fragmentary— imagine life without relief from all that has ever happened! Thus consciousness, rather than primarily adding to the store of events, instead must recurrently eliminate all that is extraneous to current requirements.[14] It is an eliminative, suppressive memory as much as it is a recalling of events; memory disposes of surplus baggage as efficiently as possible while continuously raising or restraining other kinds of potentially useful events, experiences, and evocations. And all this to what result? Certainly not a self, fully contained and complete. The idea of a continuous, linked, and teleological path misrepresents memory as much as it misunderstands duration.

How then can Bergson begin to explain how memory works, to describe the mobile and transitory states that form the basis of our selves? He used layers, or "planes," to describe memory (and selves). Memory operates as a conjoined series of perceptions, experiences, and imaginings; what we think, experience, and feel collaborate and reinforce at a variety of levels.[15] When memory occurs (which it always does), different planes of knowledge and experience intersect one another. Some of these will be explicit and conscious; others will register only with introspection and self-awareness; still others will be altogether instinctive and virtual. All together, they create what we perceive as a unified experience (and a unified self), but that ostensible cohesion belies the multiplicity which formed it.[16]

Even within memory, separate intensities and remembrances coexist. Take reading itself: you have learned to read at some point and you likely read better than many others who can read (that is, you take less time to sound out words or look up unfamiliar terms). Yet actively remembering *how to read* would impair actual reading, as well as confuse your memory of what you are reading. Indeed, you were likely unaware of the nature of your reading until a moment ago, as it had passed from what Bergson calls "recollection memory" to "habit memory." Are you conscious of reading? Yes and no: yes, as you are not repressing your memory of reading practices in a Freudian sense, but also no, as you are not thinking at a level of how-to-read, but instead what-I-am-reading. Finally, when your imagination engages with reading, you create meanings and experiences as the text becomes "yours"; when it does not (as any overworked undergraduate can attest) your eyes merely note subsequent words without forming them into larger ideas, and your moments of reading never coalesce into anything more.

Thus the experiences in which it seems that you are "merely acting" or "merely remembering" are in fact acutely amalgamated with one another, and the usual philosophical differentiation between them is manifestly wrong. Frédéric Worms calls this Bergson's "second fundamental thesis":

> We must replace the hypothesis of a single level of representations which are connected to each other through a horizontal work of association with that of a plurality of levels of representations, connected to each other through a vertical work of interpretation or comprehension.[17]

Ultimately, Bergson focused his philosophical inquiry on the various levels by which we work, which could collectively be called memory, consciousness, or "the self." But it is the work, not the abstraction doing the work, which deserves these names.

As many Bergsonians have pointed out, such an approach posits a serious disjuncture within memory and the self, without minimizing either. The self therefore has "access to novelty" without reducing all novelty to the self, what Levinas called in his discussion of Bergson (and elsewhere) "the ontology of the Same."[18] The "interpretation and comprehension" mentioned by Worms is not merely a matter of applying the correct meanings. Bergson abominates predetermination. True creativity and innovation take place here; memory and creation inextricably connect.

Bergson's conception of memory far exceeds that of formal logical formulae and representation. Memory and existence cannot be understood abstractly;

they must be approached "in terms of a plurality of planes (a plane of action, a plane of recollection, a plane of dreams, etc.)."[19] This pluralization of memory allows a better and more complex understanding of life, but also makes the discussion of such complexity more difficult; what kind of metaphysics, after all, can encompass such variety and intricacy?

If reality is mobile, then the act of abstracting ideas and concepts—both of which are fixed and inflexible—excludes reality from thought. For Bergson, memory and duration require certain forms of mental experience that exceed generally accepted philosophical thought. He called these approaches *intuition*, which neither exists separately from thought nor is identical to it. Unlike analysis, which he said "operates on immobility, intuition is located in mobility or, what amounts to the same thing, duration."[20] Intuition encompasses thought and instinct, self and other, wholeness and multiplicity. For Bergson, intuiting towers over other forms of understanding.

## Together and Apart

The linkages between James's and Bergson's pluralisms may be clear at this point. But their respective conceptions did not evolve in isolation. James and Bergson interacted creatively, responding to one another's ideas, and thus developed innovations and new understandings. While James did so more explicitly at first, Bergson lived many years longer (until 1941) and continued to develop his theories, often specifically using James as a foundation.

The connections between the two were explicitly recognized by both, and by the philosophical community at large. James, for his part, never ceased praising Bergson, for example calling *Creative Evolution* the "absolutely divinest book on philosophy ever written up to this date."[21] In letters to Bergson, James constantly and repeatedly commended his work; in letters to others, he continued to praise Bergson.[22] Perhaps most importantly, Bergson holds pride of place in *A Pluralistic Universe*. Indeed, James overcame his original difficulties in composing the series of lectures that would later form the book, he noted, by using Bergson.[23] "Reading his works," James wrote, "has made me bold."[24]

Shortly before delivering the Oxford lectures that would make up *A Pluralistic Universe*, James wrote to Bergson, "I feel that at bottom we are fighting the same fight, you a commander, I in the ranks."[25] The structure of the lectures and chapters evoked the same message: in the first five, James poses philosophical difficulties, particularly those drawn from Hegel and Fechner, and Bergson arrives in the sixth to solve them. James embraced Bergson's concepts of time and memory as a devastating critique of *intellectualism*, similar to his own anti-Hegelianism.

Bergson, for his part, became convinced that James shared his philosophical aspirations, especially after reading *Pragmatism* in 1907. He wrote to James, "you give the very formula of the metaphysics which I am convinced we will come to...."[26] His appreciation of his role in *A Pluralistic Universe* was intense; he wrote that "never before have I been examined, understood, penetrated in such a manner."[27] And in his introduction to *Pragmatism*'s translation, Bergson positioned James as a fellow traveler who had discovered the same truths he had: that "relations are fluctuating and ... things fluid."[28] He summarized James's overall project in the same language he used for his own epistemology:

> if reality does not form a single whole, if it is multiple and mobile, made up of cross-currents, truth which arises from contact with one of these currents— truth felt before being conceived—is more capable of seizing and storing up reality than truth merely thought.[29]

For Bergson, each was, in his own way, creating the future of philosophy. These new paths to a more holistic truth, would result in a "positive metaphysics" he argued, "one that is susceptible of progressing indefinitely, instead of being entirely taken or left, like the old systems."[30]

Such metaphysics cannot be foreclosed nor be teleological. The development of truth, in this view, must occur along a variety of roads using various methodologies. And these philosophies explain certain operations for subjects as diverse as truth, selves, and the universe. Each of these, in James's or Bergson's hands, turns out to operate pluralistically and to exceed that which can fit into any particular system.

To argue that, in Bergson's summary, "We invent the truth to utilize reality," meant not that truth is inconsistent (for it could not well utilize reality if it were) but that it is—most importantly—subjectively particularist: Each person works through some of the infinitely possible truths that the world throws up. This particularism attacked many of the foundational ideas in philosophy, as metaphysicians of the time well understood. Similarly, the debates over the Jamesian conception of pragmatism were well underway throughout the first decade of the twentieth century. His central idea that truths are what we use, rather than ideal forms which exist independently of human experience, had already become as controversial and misrepresented as it has remained since then.

Each pluralized the self as well. Bergson's discussion of memory makes clear the multiplicity of the individual in his thought. Even a decade before he began to use the term *pluralism*, James's *Principles of Psychology* had argued for the multiplicity of the individual. Critics noted the similarity: many accused Bergson of deriving his philosophy from James's.[31] Much of James's early psychological work had insisted on the continuity and variation of consciousness. By 1910, in one of his final essays, James argued that consciousness itself should not be conceptualized as either unitary or differentiated, as it consists of "a mass of present sensation, in a cloud of memories, emotions, concepts, etc." He called this a "field," echoing Bergson's "planes," and emphasized its temporal nature: each feeling "came out of its predecessor and will melt into its successor as continuously again. . . ."[32] In *A Pluralistic Universe*, he made clear the excessive and fundamentally indescribable (that is, impossible to fully "intellectualize") nature of all moments of being: "Every smallest state of consciousness, concretely taken, overflows its own definition."[33]

Neither man ultimately supported the idea of the singularity of the universe, yet both pointed far more to life within it than did other nonmaterialist philosophers. Bergson argued that, contrary to our desire to think of the universe as either eternal or divine in creation (or both), the universe exists as overlapping and ensuing events, such as changing, acting, and growing. "It is no longer then of the universe in its totality that we must speak."[34] Instead, we should recognize that, though a situation or law may seem natural and thus universal to us, it not only could be different elsewhere, but also may be altered by new situations that emerge from growth and change. James, in his turn, preferred to speak of the "multiverse" which makes up a "'universe'; for every part, tho it may not be in actual or immediate connexion, is nevertheless in some possible or mediated connexion, with every other part however remote."[35] Multiplicity and connection are the same, for James; the aim for absolutism and unity creates distance and difference as problems. This is not Leibniz's idealistic integration, he points out, but a "strung-along type, the type of continuity, contiguity, or concatenation."[36]

James saw his modes and methodologies as increasingly combined with Bergson's. Toward the beginning of their correspondence, he wrote to Bergson of his intent to write a book on metaphysics "which in many of its fundamental ideas agrees closely with what you have set forth. . . ."[37] Yet James was not above rhetorical slight-of-hand to make clear the connections between his thought and Bergson's. In the appendix to *A Pluralistic Universe*, he drew out an extended parallel between Bergson's approaches and those of his close friend (and founder of pragmatism) Charles Pierce. Pointing out the similarities between Bergson's denials of universal, unchanging axioms and Piercean probability theory, James argued that both ultimately share the same view of newness and creation: it is never created wholesale, but arrives in qualitatively important but empirically minute changes.[38]

Suggesting that either James or Bergson considered these questions strictly "philosophical" would be misleading, however. For the openness by both to religious experience and supernaturalism bespeaks a further connection between them and a similarity of their outlooks. The ultimate test of empirical pluralism is an acceptance of the possibility, even the likelihood, that others' experiences have a measure of legitimacy, even if those experiences make no "sense."

This openness has been long used to discredit the theoretical developments of both thinkers; how, it is asked, can we take seriously formulations of thoughts that make room for ghosts, séances, and divine intervention in human affairs? Yet what, after all, is the divine but an everyday explanation for things that make little sense? And while science seems to displace the divine, James argued that a scientific explanation is essentially another allegorical representation of personal experience; pragmatically, scientific operations must be understood by the individual no more than myth must be. An example: in the book *The Two Sources of Morality and Religion*, Bergson quoted an extended passage from William James. In the excerpt, from *The Principles of Psychology*, James tells of visiting Stanford University. Before his visit, a friend tells him to beware of California's earthquakes, so, when a temblor awakens James one morning, he is thrilled to have acquaintance with his friend's earthquake. Not only does he admire the strength of the earthquake as it occurs, but he also discovers that everyone else who experienced the event attributed it with their own versions of intention and personalization. But, then, if each sees it differently, James asks, "What was this 'It'?"[39]

Let us take in turn James's and Bergson's lessons from this story. For James, the earthquake reminds him of how impossible it would be in a theological world to reject the idea of God responding to specific acts, if even today he and others experience such an event in immediate and personal terms. For Bergson, however, the story shows how individuation leads to fragmentation: Each individual, without guidance in interpretation, will see divergent causes. This, in turn, leads to Bergson's focus on mystics, within Christianity and others, who create commonality of meaning of experience and break down invidious competitions.[40] For both, the plurality of experience leads to calls for supranatural explanation, though for James there remains little need for that explanation to be collective.

## Impressions

Lines of influence, as James argued, are hard to track precisely—such a large number exist, and act in such multiplicitious ways, that drawing connections can never be an absolute project. To trace Bergson's influence on French philosophy for the next century, even if that influence remains little recognized in English, is also to trace James's. The connections between the two thinkers, their mutually constituted recognition that truth and thought often have lacunae between them, echo throughout the century that followed them.[41]

For the first decades of the twentieth century, Bergson was widely regarded as the most important philosopher in France, if not the world. And yet the public and academic recognition of his influence has steadily declined, revived only in recent years. Even within his lifetime, Bergson's insights stopped seeming particularly original, in part because they thoroughly saturated the time's conceptions. The emergence of phenomenology neglected its own roots in Bergson's insistence that bodies exist in motion; at times, European phenomenologists even quoted James with more approval than they were willing to extend to Bergson.[42] Existentialism preferred to emphasize Nietzsche's and Heidegger's ostensible rejection of metaphysics rather than recognizing its similarities to Bergson's privileging of existences over essences. And the overall desire of philosophers to develop systematic and all-encompassing theoretical systems left little room for theorists whose ideas overtly rejected such systematization.

Yet Bergson never entirely disappeared. One cannot overemphasize his influence on Merleau-Ponty, who was elected to Bergson's chair in Modern Philosophy at the Collège de France and seemed "Bergson's most faithful and original interpreter."[43] Georg Lukács became fascinated with Bergson (and with the German Bergsonian Georg Simmel) and utilized his language to criticize Taylorist principles of fixing and organizing time.[44] Heidegger used many of Bergson's insights about the complexity and unity of being in his work. And the very foundations of phenomenology and existentialism, for all their differences, emphasized temporality and privileged experience over idealization; Bergson had helped make these acceptable philosophical inquiries. Indeed, today's tendency for French thinkers to regard philosophy as "supple, living, and human" bears the mark of Bergson.[45]

Nor did those outside philosophy entirely forget him. Marcel Proust, whose cousin married Bergson, used a Bergsonian conception of memory in *Remembrance of Things Past*. Bergson's influence on the major European art movements of the early twentieth century, namely fauvism, cubism, and futurism, were thoroughly acknowledged by the artists themselves.[46] A misguided, anti-Semitic professor ridicules both Bergson and Einstein in James Joyce's *Finnegans Wake*.[47] A considerable percentage of the period's theoretically inclined authors and artists continued Bergson's legacy outside and beyond the boundaries of academic philosophy.

Bergson's most important legatee of the late twentieth century was Gilles Deleuze. In an early essay on Bergson (1956) and a later monograph (1966), Deleuze found in Bergson a motivation for a new kind of philosophy, an approach emphasizing pluralities of being instead of building correlations or developing homogeneity. "There was," Deleuze said in retrospect, something in him that could not be assimilated, which enabled him to provide a shock, to be a rallying point for all the opposition, the object of so many hatreds: and this is not so much because of the theme of duration, as of the theory and practice of becomings of all kinds, of coexistent multiplicities.[48]

Inspired in part by his own reading of Bergson, Deleuze developed a conception of pluralism as central to his own philosophical concerns. For Deleuze, the sources of identity and action proliferate endlessly, and the philosopher's proper role is to encourage this expansive creation. Much of his later, more famous work, developed from combining these Bergsonian concepts with other theoretical and political trajectories. Deleuze found in Bergson the inspiration of difference: making disparate overabundance central to evolutionary and intellectual creativity, allowing for new concepts and approaches. Bergson, he said, showed that "If difference itself is biological, consciousness of difference is historical."[49] This provides the potential for divergent kinds of philosophical investigations: Deleuze's interests are those philosophers who bestow deviations rather than systems, networks rather than straits, options rather than compulsions.

Bergsonian pluralisms pervade Deleuze's writings, from his solo projects to his overtly political work with Felix Guattari. Deleuze and Guattari built the notion of the "rhizome" from Bergson's *Creative Evolution*: rhizomes develop not through units which determine those which come after them (the arboreal model of evolution), but through "variation, expansion, conquest, capture, offshoots."[50] In *A Thousand Plateaus*, the authors entitle one section "Memories of a Bergsonian." Elsewhere, they take almost verbatim Bergson's phrase "places of flight" to identify those corporeal and intellectual locales where new connections, transitions, and creations are built.[51] Finally, Deleuze's books on cinema are themselves specific and conscious attempts to work through Bergson's concepts of motion, duration, memory, and time.[52] In all of these attempts, Deleuze followed Bergson in "one of the least appreciated aspects of his thought—the constitution of a logic of multiplicities."[53]

This is not to argue that Deleuze is somehow fundamentally a Jamesian; such reductionism impoverishes the richness and differences between both philosophical approaches. But two important approaches result. First, this underscores certain similarities between them, such as their anti-foundationalism, their foci on tendencies and intensities rather than certainties and closures, and their respective tychistic pluralisms. Second, and more significantly, contextualizing these philosophies within their intellectual histories, separated by almost a century, makes clear that neither did they emerge in a vacuum nor are they unrelated. Both those who treat James or Bergson as unimportant traditional figures, and those who dismiss Deleuze as indiscriminate or haphazard, ignore the complex developments that comprise philosophical thought. Such readings are intrinsically ahistorical and thus reinforce boundary disputes within philosophy rather than investigating what seemingly different branches can say to one another.

Other Jamesian engenderings could also be drawn between European and American influences. Though James's friendship and intellectual affiliation with Bergson had profound and long-term effects in Continental philosophy, it was not only through Bergson that James influenced Europeans. For example, the art historians Marianne Teuber and Eliza Jane Reilly present inconclusive but significant evidence suggesting James's influence among European artists.[54] While Teuber circumstantially links Pablo Picasso to Jamesian ideas (predominantly through James's student Gertrude Stein), Reilly provocatively constructs connections between James's psychological pluralism and early European modernism in general. And T. E. Hulme, the famous essayist of modernism, declared shortly after James's death, "I am a pluralist." He continued, "There is no Unity, no Truth, but forces which have different aims, and whose whole reality consists in those differences."[55]

Nor were James's transatlantic effects limited to Western Europe. As evinced by recent scholarship, James had a complex relationship with Russia, a complementary influence until recently obscured by Soviet (and anti-Soviet) readings of philosophical history. James's renown rose swiftly and widely: virtually unknown before the turn of the century, he was elected to the Moscow Psychological Society in 1901. The second of his major books translated into Russian, *The Varieties of Religious Experience*, went through five printings in 1910, its first year of publication.[56] The same year, the keynote speaker at the Moscow Psychological Society's twenty-fifth inaugural celebration asserted James's preeminence and claimed that the "future of philosophy belonged to pragmatism."[57]

Part of this had to do with a form of *fin de siècle* anti-positivist mysticism emerging in Russian student culture, within which James, like Nietzsche, led toward a world beyond the sterility of science.[58] Part also had to do with the disparate strains of theological and spiritual components of Russian modernism, such as the Russian Symbolists' fascination with theosophy.[59] But much also had to do with the Russians' interest in the possibilities of James's pluralistic outlook, which seemed to them to solve a number of philosophical conundrums.

The disappearance of James's thought from Russian intellectual history had an unequivocal cause. For Lenin, of course, pluralism was inadmissible; one could not doubt what actions to take, nor admit to more than one possibly right approach. James, accordingly, was only one more in a line of American anti-revolutionaries.[60] The subsequent years saw James's thought incrementally misrepresented in the history of Russian thought as merely pro-religious, proto-capitalist, and (most surprisingly) propounding imperialism.[61] Interestingly, the earliest post-Soviet dismissal of James, in the pivotal journal *Under the Banner of Socialism*, associated James closely with Bergson in dismissing him as anti-logical.[62] By mid-century, the previous associations between James and Russian philosophy and psychology had vanished.

Central and Western Europe had their share of Jamesian psychologists and pragmatic philosophers as well. James was in close contact with Italians who formed the "Florentine Pragmatic Club."[63] More than half of the books on pragmatism published by 1925, Reilly reports, were European, with England, Germany, Italy, France, Spain, Poland, and the Netherlands showing an interest.[64] Thus, James's fame and influence were clear, much of it still recognized by contemporary historians. Yet those acknowledgments of his European intellectual influence mention only his dated psychological work and overt pragmatism. The last section of this chapter asks why, after all this, do current American and European philosophers, or more simply Jamesians and Bergsonians, fail to recognize the intellectual connections between us?

## Aftermath

In the subsequent century, these connections were erased, to the point where one can speak confidently of the respective traditions of Anglo-American and Continental philosophy. But this division is political as much as a geographic. For the motivations underpinning the creation of this division influence (and are influenced by) the continual recreation of both a nationalist project of autochthony on the part of the Americans and a conscious historical amnesia on the part of French thinkers.

Clear as it seemed to their contemporaries, James's connection to Bergson faded as dramatically as his Russian connections, to the point where their relationship passes entirely unremarked in most of today's portrayals of his thought. Following James's death, the similarities between his work and Bergson's (and that of Continental philosophers in general) were downplayed by his followers in the United States. James, they felt, should be *sui generis*, and debts to others (even those he himself expressed) undermined his originality. "Society's most precious products are its undisciplinables," wrote Horace Kallen, one of the most indefatigable of James's students. "Its most creative and masterful dynamic forces are its *unaccountable* geniuses."[65]

Kallen argued, therefore, that James and Bergson had radically different approaches, and that James's was the work of a true visionary. While admitting that, to the untrained eye, Bergson may seem "democratic and pluralistic" and that he properly "acknowledges the consubstantiality of every item of experience," Kallen contended that Bergson ultimately fails to stand up against James in almost all ways, resulting in a philosophically universal dogmatism which creates an "inert and powerless" world.[66] At one point, Bergson's arguments are merely a warmed-over transcendentalism, whereas the "main outlines of James's thought are not prefigured in the history of philosophy."[67] In another stance, Kallen argued that Bergson holds to a conception like all other philosophers before him, unlike James's overcoming of intellectual history. Bergson, unlike James, "is before all things systematic, consistently architechtonic, a monist who insists on an irrefragable difference between appearance and reality...."[68] To add insult, he also mentions in passing how much easier Bergson's writings are to understand than are James's (an opinion noticeably—and warrantedly—absent in any other comparison of the two theorists).[69]

Kallen was not alone in trying to differentiate the two methods and philosophies. James's friend Théodore Flournoy and the writer Walter Pitkin noted important similarities between the two but also primarily emphasized their differences.[70] And those who came later continued in the separation, until very little of their affiliation was noted at all, except in the negative. Virtually no encyclopedias of philosophy, for example, even suggest an overlap between Bergson and James, and those latter-day theorists who have been interested in one rarely take the other seriously. A recent example: Louis Menand's popular rendition of the history of pragmatism's emergence, which entirely avoids substantive mention of Bergson (or just about any European influences).[71]

Clearly, important differences between the two modes of thought must be taken into account. But what is so vitally at stake that James's readers must renounce aspects of his inspiration and contradict James's own statements of intellectual connection? Some of the effects of James's thought—the contention that ideas must be masculinely robust and self-sustaining, for example—clearly undermined the pluralist recognition of interrelated engagement.[72] Similarly, the common desire to analyze (and heroize) philosophers in isolation from one another and their historical influences affects James's readers as much as anyone. But U.S. exceptionalism also looms here: it was impossible that a great (even *the* great) American philosopher, perhaps the first one to stand up to the tyranny of European philosophy, could have been truly inspired and guided by a popular exemplar of that tradition. Thus, the defense of James necessitated for many a rejection of these Continental lines of influence, lest their hero (and by extension their American selves) be diminished.

Europeans, on the contrary, emphasized the connection between the two to a far greater extent. The perceived connection between Bergson and American pluralism, pragmatism, and radical empiricism continued well into the emergence of existentialism. James was widely read in Europe, and the parallels between his psychology and Bergson's theories of time and memory seemed much clearer there, perhaps even too clear. Even during James's lifetime, Bergson felt misrepresented as being dependent on James, to the extent that he wrote in to the *Revue Philosophique* to correct a claim that his book *Time and Free Will* was inspired in part by James.[73] (This contention was a matter of great debate in Bergson's time: it is unlikely that Bergson had read James's work, given the lack of French translation and the absence of debate about James by the book's publication date.[74])

But by the end of his life, Bergson embraced the connection: he overtly referred to James's influence on his thought and referred extensively to the American's life and work in his own. He used James's examples and theories in his own writings, and continued to champion the American to a French audience. Indeed, Bergson kept a picture of James over his work desk, one that remains in its museological mummification to this day.

European recognition of the James–Bergson connection dissipated only as Bergson's fame faded. The eclipse of Bergson by debates over communism and the embrace of existentialism, as well as the emergence of positivist models of social thought, made his inspirations and influence increasingly uninteresting and immaterial to French thought. Nor did the circumstances of Bergson's death make for comforting history in France—he died from an illness contracted while standing in the rain to be registered as a Jew under the Vichy regime. Bergson's diminishment actually came in part through his connections to James. French critics often attacked Bergson through his Jamesianism; a negative review of James's work was implicitly understood to assail the tides of Bergsonian influence. Durkheim, for example, deplored James's alleged antipathy to rationalism, a criticism generally understood to be attacking Bergson's anti-rationalism more than James's pragmatism.[75] Debates as to whether or not Bergson was a "radical empiricist," a Jamesian term never employed by Bergson, continued far beyond the death of both.[76]

Thus the severing of Bergson's and James's thought, so thoroughly reinforced in the United States, occurred only minimally in France. But as extensive as Bergson's influences were at the beginning of the century, the memory and study of his thought nonetheless slowly disappeared from the scene of Continental philosophy. The Bergson–James connection—indeed, the entire *fin de siècle* period of substantial overlap and influence between American and French thought—thus became obscured by the equally important differences which predated this connection and developed from it.

But lines of influence remain. Conscious acknowledgment, as James and other psychologists of his time pointed out, is far from the only form of motivation and inspiration in human endeavors. Insofar as James was an American philosopher, he was a European philosopher, too. Insomuch as Bergson was the archetypal French metaphysician of his time, he was an American thinker as well. The building of walls between the two, the ignorance and eradication of the overlaps between their intellectual projects and their historical influence, comes at a price. The proper pluralistic projects of philosophy are replaced with purity, absolutism, and a deluded conception of radical distance.

And this distance comprises the return of the absolutism that James's pluralism intended to displace. The insistence of purity, of the clear demarcation of intellectual history, serves to depoliticize and decontaminate the project of national thought. By drawing clear walls between differing traditions and denying mutual inspiration, exemplarity and native genius can better serve as stand-ins for national character. If America's intellectual genealogy is untainted by European influence, so much the better for America. Nothing is owed, since nothing was given, and nothing was taken. If postmodernism has infected our shores, it can be represented as the thoughts of foreigners, profoundly distant from the moderate and pragmatic American tradition. If students are being taught Deleuze or Foucault, it can be argued that they are being turned against their scholarly birthright. This is possible only when a great American thinker like William James is one of us, not one of them. The alternative—that we are part of them, and they are part of us—can remain unthought.

## Notes

1. Anyone interested in following up these approaches could consult: Alan Sokal and Jean Bricmont, *Fashionable Nonsense: Postmodern Intellectuals and the Abuse of Science* (New York: Picador, 1999); Seyla Benhabib, Judith Butler, Drucilla Cornell, and Nancy Fraser, *Feminist Contentions: A Philosophical Exchange* (New York: Routledge, 1995); *Just Being Difficult? Academic Writing in the Public Arena*, ed. Jonathan Culler and Brian Lamb (Stanford, CA: Stanford University Press, 2003); and Roger Kimball, *Tenured Radicals: How Politics Has Corrupted Our Higher Education* (New York: HarperCollins, 1990) if he or she were inclined (against counsel) to do so.

2. Of course, similar arguments have been made elsewhere: Most intellectual historians accept Emerson's influence on Nietzsche, or acknowledge Pierce's on French semiotics. But too often even these acknowledgments become struggles for recognition ("Look! We Americans influenced Nietzsche!") rather than an attention to the interrelationships of intellectual trajectories.

3. Henri Bergson, "On the Pragmatism of William James: Truth and Reality," trans. Melissa McMahon, in *Key Writings*, ed. Keith Ansell Pearson and John Mullarkey (New York: Continuum, 2002), p. 267.

4. Henri Bergson, *Creative Evolution*, trans. Arthur Mitchell (New York: Henry Holt and Co., 1911), pp. 50–51.

5. Bergson, *Creative Evolution*, p. 4.

6. Bergson, *Creative Evolution*, p. 308 (emphasis in original).

7. Bergson, *Creative Evolution*, p. 310.

8. F. C. T. Moore terms this use of intuition "thinking backwards" to highlight the central role of multiple durations in thought. *Bergson: Thinking Backwards* (Cambridge, UK: Cambridge University Press, 1996).

9. Gilles Deleuze, *Bergsonism*, trans. Hugh Tomplinson and Barbara Habberjam (New York: Zone Books, 1988), 42 (emphasis in original).

10. Timothy S. Murphy, "Beneath Relativity," *The New Bergson*, ed. John Mullarkey (Manchester, UK: Manchester University Press, 1999), p. 77 (emphases in original).

11. Henri Bergson, *Introduction to Metaphysics*, trans. Mabelle L. Andison (New York: Wisdom Library, 1961), p. 73.

12. William Faulkner, *Requiem for a Nun*, 1959, Act I, Scene III.

13. Deleuze, *Bergsonism*, p. 63.

14. This is the central thesis of Marie Cariou's essay "Bergson: The Keyboards of Forgetting," trans. Melissa McMahon, in Mullarkey, *The New Bergson*, pp. 91–117.

15. Henri Bergson, *Matter and Memory*, trans. Nancy Margaret Paul and W. Scott Palmer (London: Allen and Unwin, 1911).

16. See, e.g., Bergson, *Matter and Memory*, p. 323–24.

17. Frédéric Worms, "*Matter and Memory* on Mind and Body," in Mullarkey, *The New Bergson*, pp. 93–94.

18. Emmanuel Levinas, *Time and the Other*, trans. Richard A. Cohen (Pittsburgh: Duquesne University Press, 1987), p. 132.

19. Keith Ansell Pearson, *Philosophy and the Adventure of the Virtual: Bergson and the Time of Life* (London: Routledge, 2002), p. 171.

20. Bergson, *Introduction to Metaphysics*, p. 43.

21. Quoted by John J. McDermott in his Introduction to James's *Essays in Philosophy* (Cambridge, MA: Harvard University Press, 1978), p. xxxi.

22. McDermott, Introduction to James's *Essays in Philosophy*, p. xxxii.

23. James wrote to F. C. S. Schiller, on February 14, 1908, "Came into clear water rē Oxford lectures–Bergson helping." *APU*, p. 215.

24. *APU*, p. 97.

25. June 13, 1907, letter, quoted in Richard J. Bernstein's "Introduction" in *APU*, p. xxii.

26. Letter of June 27, 1907, in *Mélanges*, p. 361.

27. Letter of July 23, 1908, *Mélanges*, p. 363.

28. "On the Pragmatism . . . ," p. 268.

29. "On the Pragmatism . . . ," p. 273.

30. Letter of February 15, 1905, in *Mélanges*, p. 361.

31. G. Rageot, "5th International Congress of Psychology," *Revue Philosophique de la France et de l'Etranger* 60, no. 1, pp. 84–85. Bergson writes in to the journal to rebut this, as discussed below. See *Mélanges*, p. 387, note 30.

32. James, *Essays in Philosophy*, p. 158.

33. *APU*, p. 129.

34. Bergson, *Creative Evolution*, p. 241.

35. *APU*, p. 146.

36. *APU*, p. 147.

37. December 14, 1902, letter, quoted in Bernstein, "Introduction," p. xii.

38. *APU*, p. 151–54.

39. William James, *Essays in Psychology* (Cambridge, MA: Harvard University Press, 1983), pp. 331–38; quoted (and translated by) Bergson in *The Two Sources of Morality and Religion*, trans. R. Ashely Audra and Cloudesley Brereton (New York: Henry Holt, 1935).

40. P. A. Y. Gunter sees this move toward commonality within diversity as a source of meaning for environmentalism. See his "Bergson and the War against Nature," in *The New Bergson*, pp. 168–72.

41. Frédéric Worms, "James et Bergson: Lectures Croisées," *Philosophie* no. 64 (1999), pp. 54–68.

42. Cf. Michael Tavuzzi, "A Note on Husserl's Dependence on William James," *Journal of the British Society for Phenomenology* 10, no. 3 (October 1979), p. 194–96.

43. Richard A. Cohen, "Philo, Spinoza, Bergson: Rise of an Ecological Age," in *The New Bergson*, p. 28.

44. Lucio Colletti, *Marxism and Hegel*, trans. Lawrence Garner (London: Verso, 1979), esp. chapter 10.

45. Bergson, in "La Philosophie Français," *La Revue de Paris*, III (1915), quoted in Ben-Ami Scharfstein, *Roots of Bergson's Philosophy* (New York: Columbia University Press, 1943).

46. Mark Antliff, *Inventing Bergson: Cultural Politics and the Parisian Avant-Garde* (Princeton, NJ: Princeton University Press, 1993).

47. James Joyce, *Finnegans Wake* (London: Penguin, 1976), p. 149. See also Dominic Manganiello, *Joyce's Politics* (London: Routledge and Kegan Paul, 1981), p. 230.

48. Gilles Deleuze and Claire Parnet, *Dialogues*, trans. Hugh Tomlinson and Barbara Hammerjam (London: Althone, 1987), p. 15, also quoted in *Bergsonism*, p. 8.

49. Gilles Deleuze, "Bergson's Conception of Difference," in *The New Bergson*, p. 51. The essay can also be found in slightly expanded form in *Les Études Bergsoniennes* 4 (1956), pp. 79–112.

50. Keith Ansell-Pearson makes this point in his essay "Bergson and Creative Evolution/Involution," *The New Bergson*, esp. pp. 157–63. The quotation itself is from Deleuze and Guattari, *A Thousand Plateaus: Capitalism and Schizophrenia*, trans. Brian Massumi (Minneapolis: University of Minnesota Press, 1987), p. 21.

51. Letter to James, January 6, 1902, *Mélanges*, 355. Though the letter is written in French, this phrase is in English.

52. Gilles Deleuze, *Cinema 1: The Movement-Image*, trans. Hugh Tomlinson and Barbara Habberjam (London: Athlone, 1986), and *Cinema 2: The Time-Image*, trans. Hugh Tomlinson and Robert Galeta (London: Athlone, 1988).

53. *Bergsonism*, p. 117.

54. Marianne L. Teuber, "Gertrude Stein, William James, and Pablo Picasso's Cubism" in *A Pictorial History of Psychology*, ed. Wolfgang G. Bringmann, Helmut E. Luck, Rudolf Miller, and Charles E. Early, (Chicago: Quintessence Publishing, 1997), pp. 256–64; Eliza Jane Reilly, "Concrete Possibilities: William James and the European Avant-Garde," *Streams of William James* 2, no. 3, pp. 22–29.

55. Quoted in Christopher Butler, *Early Modernism: Literature, Music and Painting in Europe, 1900–1916* (Oxford, UK: Oxford University Press, 1994), p. 209.

56. Gennady Obatnin, "James and Viacheslav Ivanov at the 'Threshold of Consciousness,'" in *William James and Russian Culture*, ed. Joan Delany Grossman and Ruth Rischin (Lanhan, MD: Lexington, 2003), p. 123.

57. Randall A. Poole, "William James in the Moscow Psychological Society: Pragmatism, Pluralism, Personalism," in *William James and Russian Culture*, ed. Grossman and Rischin, pp. 133–34. The speech, Lev Lopatin's "The Present and Future of Philosophy," is cited by Poole at "Nastoiashchee i budushchee filosofi," *Voprosy Filososofii i Psikhologii* 21, no. 3 (1910), pp. 263–305.

58. See Joan Delany Grossman, "Philosophers, Decadents, and Mystics: James's Russian Readers in the 1890s," in *William James and Russian Culture*, ed. Grossman and Rischin, pp. 93–111.

59. Obatnin, "James and Viacheslav Ivanov," p. 113–29.

60. V. I. Lenin, *Materialism and Empiriocriticism*, trans. Abraham Fineburg (Moscow: Progress Publishers), chapter 6, sec. 4.

61. Joan Delany Grossman and Ruth Rischin, "Introduction," to *William James and Russian Culture*, ed. Grossman and Rischin, pp. 7–9.

62. Grossman and Rischin, "Introduction," p. 7.

63. William James, "G. Papini and the Pragmatist Movement in Italy," *Essays in Philosophy* (Cambridge, MA: Harvard University Press, 1978), pp. 144–48.

64. Reilly, "Concrete Possibilities," p. 23.

65. Horace Kallen, *William James and Henri Bergson: A Study in Contrasting Theories of Life* (Chicago: University of Chicago Press, 1914), p. 234 (italics mine).

66. Kallen, *William James and Henri Bergson*, p. 35.

67. Kallen, *William James and Henri Bergson*, p. 177.

68. Kallen, *William James and Henri Bergson*, p. 104.

69. Kallen, *William James and Henri Bergson*, p. viii.

70. Flournoy, *The Philosophy of William James*; Emile Boutroux, *William James* (New York: Longman's, Green, 1912); Walter Boughton Pitkin, "James and Bergson; Or, Who is Against Intellect?" *Journal of Philosophy, Psychology, and Scientific Method* 7, no. 9 (1910), pp. 225–31.

71. Louis Menand, *The Metaphysical Club: A Story of Ideas in America* (New York: Farrar, Straus, and Giroux, 2001). Note Menand's implicit thesis regarding U.S. exceptionalism in the title, in a book with more than one chapter devoted to pluralism.

72. Townsend, *Manhood at Harvard: William James and Others* (New York: W. W. Norton, 1996).

73. See his letter of July 20, 1905 to James, in Henri Bergson, *Key Writings*, pp. 360–61. The letter appears in *Revue Philosophique de la France et de l'Etranger* 60, no. 2 (August 1905), pp. 229–30.

74. See Ben-Ami Scharfstein's *Roots of Bergson's Philosophy* (New York: Columbia University Press, 1943), pp. 29–32.

75. Introduction to Emile Durkheim, *Pragmatism and Sociology*, trans. J. C. Whitehouse, intro. John B. Allcock (Cambridge, UK: Cambridge University Press, 1983).

76. Milič Čapek, *Bergson and Modern Physics: A Reinterpretation and Re-evaluation* (Dordrect: Reidel, 1971).

# 5

# Onticology Recapitulates Philosophy

> Originally—so much is sure—things themselves had a personality and an inherent power.
>
> —Marcel Mauss, *Essai sur le Don*[1]

John Boodin, a student and colleague of William James, told the following story in memory of his teacher:

> Some of us had been listening to a noted preacher [Lyman Abbott]. . . . We were profoundly impressed by his appeal that worthiness of immortality was the important thing rather than the fact of immortality. We walked home with William James, and he invited us into his study. He asked questions and one of us grew very eloquent in defense of the abstract worthiness of immortality. James' reply was characteristic. He fastened upon us his benignant smile and said: "Which would you rather: to be worthy of a fine beautiful wife or to have one?" It silenced the argument, for . . . it brought home to us that the best things in life are not abstractions. They come as gifts and raise us by their coming.[2]

As immediately entertaining as this story is (and as insightful as James's rebuke of Abbott's privileging of desert over achievement is, as well), three parts of Boodin's account evoke important aspects of James's theoretical approach. The first, and perhaps the most immediately striking to those looking back on such a quotation, concerns the readiness of James and his interlocutors to conflate a "wife" with the category "desirable object."[3] The second, a position commonly attributed to James and a well-understood central tenet for pragmatism in general, shows that theological verities are trumped by individual preferences and that one cannot truly compel forms of belief by abstractions. The third, and for my purposes here the most interesting, reflects the role that "things," as Boodin calls them, are the philosophical corrective to academic error. Things, here, not only help make sense of the flaws of abstract argument, but define a more productive intellectual inquiry.

For in this story, as in philosophy, the generalized realm of truth becomes contested and engaged not through some kind of pure realm of thought, but by examining how humans interact with the material world. James takes the abstraction of an appealing argument and, standing it up against the reality of human desire, identifies not the logical flaw in Abbott's argument but the privileges of the physical over the mental. *Things*, hereby, make philosophy.

### A. Philosophical Things

In James's own conceptualization, this relation distances things from the ideas they generate. Through philosophy (and through science) things disappear just as they are used to ground reality. "The 'things' are not invisible impalpable things," he writes, or else "the whole *naif* conception of thing gets superseded, and a thing's name is interpreted as denoting only the law or *regel der verbindung* by which certain of our sensations habitually succeed or coexist."[4]

This chapter asks how this comes to be. First, what are the relationships between our thoughts (namely, their epistemological formulation as philosophy) and things, and how and why do we theorize about things? Second, why is philosophy so imbedded in the things it denies? What is the history of this emergence and how has this relationship emerged? Third, and finally, I address the problem of things' infinities, the pluralism inherent in the very matter of physicality. What, in other words, would it mean to take seriously a Jamesian pluralism when it comes to things, and how do humans interact pluralistically with things?

### Virgil: "Sunt lacrimae rerum."[5]

The experience of a thing, the physical connection of the object and the human senses of touch, sight, taste, smell, or sound, are not precisely external. Certainly they are the boundaries of what we as physical beings can experience of the exoteric, but they also are, oddly, individualized and personal. One person's sensations translate awkwardly to another's. A flavor can be excruciating for me but spectacular for you. The realm of judgment is simultaneously particular and shared, private and politicized.[6]

Even extreme engagements with objects can take place for one person while another nearby remains uninvolved, even unaware. The effects and causes of those engagements can be purely individualistic, even while their constructions and ultimate meanings belong to the shared domains of interpretation, language, and representation. And the engagements themselves are never entirely distinct from the self—whatever sensation arises from interaction with an object is both of the self and of the object. As Elaine Scarry has pointed out, "when a knife or nail or pin enters the body, one feels not the knife, nail or pin, but one's own body, one's own body hurting one."[7] Our engagements are just that: our own.

Yet things, by their very nature, are communal. A thing that cannot be seen, felt, or heard by others cannot specifically be called a "thing"—it is, instead, a phantasm. Thus, the life of things is necessarily social.[8] Disagreement about what kind of thing a particular thing is, or over a thing's essential status (its measure, its consecration), can be nothing other than social, and therefore politicized, disagreements.

Things, in other words, must be invented, and this invention is a political process. How we come to know things, what they are, how they signify, that they even exist: all are contestable, all are socially and culturally based modes. In short, materialism matters. In *Pragmatism*, James points to the experience of a baby who, dropping a rattle and losing sight of it, also loses knowledge of its existence.[9] The idea of the thing, a thing which has continuity and permanence independent of us, is a philosophical invention, and a remarkably serviceable one. But like all inventions, James explains, it has a history and a specificity, which tend to be neglected because the concept of the thing is so useful and powerful. It "becomes an interpretation so luminous of what happens to us that, once employed, it never gets forgotten."[10]

Marx and Engels told perhaps the best-known story of the history of materialism's relationship to philosophy, likely the most convincing narrative of this emergence. In their first coauthored work, *The Holy Family*, they traced the development of English materialism through Hobbes, Duns Scotus, Locke, and Hume, while sketching French materialism from Descartes to LeRoy to Bayle.[11] Marx and Engels's interest was in opposing materialism to metaphysics: the positivism of science, they believed, was in the process of driving out the misconceptions of philosophy. The politics of things were the politics of truth; the material world would trump the metaphysical world because the former leads away from error. Materialism's result was, for them, necessarily one of the two mutually reinforcing possibilities of "natural science proper" or "socialism and communism."[12]

So though Marx and Engels historicized materialism, their teleological progression positioned *things* as the answer to metaphysics. Marx's later work in

*Capital* follows this pattern, wherein things are effects, not causes, of social relations. Marxism's politicization of materialism uses commodities to discover the truth of class conflict and identity, but things themselves are not the locus of inquiry; instead, such a materialism sees things as emblematic embodiments of the true location of politics. Note also the common, almost invisible conflation between "things" and "commodities" within Marxian approaches.

"Knowledge about a thing is not the thing itself," James reminded his readers.[13] James was not a materialist in the sense of holding that things have meaning somehow inherent within them, nor did he believe that things were a kind of key that would open the door to true reality. As Ralph Barton Perry has argued, James was not a philosopher of things; he was a philosopher of the experience of things, of the interconnected constitution of subjects and objects.[14] On the one hand, things around us (including persons) make us who we are; on the other, we decide the uses of those things, depending on what they can do and what we think we can do with them. Following Bergson, James held that "what really *exists* is not things made but things in the making."[15]

There cannot be, for James, any true unity of things, no more than there can be any true unity of selves. From early in his career as a psychologist, James argued that the individual mind, not the world itself, forms unity. Illusions, hallucinations, and other misperceptions arise from our expectations and patterns of thought. Those under anesthetic feel as though their limbs move even when they do not, for example; similarly, when one is (incorrectly) convinced that one is eating venison, the correlative flavors of venison seem to stand out.[16] Critically, it is the things themselves that force reexamination of these expectations, when the result and the anticipation differ too much. Sensations and thoughts, James held, are always and forever different; it is the mind that conjoins, organizes, and unifies them.[17]

Of course, this is not to say that consciousness must be unified. Indeed, it is against their recognition of discontinuous modes of thought that philosophers have positioned a unitary external world. For James, consciousness is better understood in the sense of what he famously called "streams," overlapping, coursing, never-static flows. These vary in intensity, in power, in kind, and in effect, but cannot be frozen in place; to do so is to take a kind of snapshot of a tiny moment, far from understanding consciousness itself.

Thus exists a direct relationship between human subjectivity/consciousness and the world of objects, though one contrary to that drawn by the great philosophical systematizers. Both the self and the objects encountered by the self operate on different registers, multiple dimensions.

> The world as given to human consciousness, the world of objects, is the world we experience because it is the correlate of a consciousness which can simultane-

ously and successively live in "different orders of reality," in the perceptual, the imaginary, the ideal, etc.[18]

Everyday objects serve both as the reference points upon which our world is built and as the unsettling divergences those worlds can take.

What, then, of the philosophical laws which underwrite things' realities? Is not the truth of a thing the way in which it is bound to universal standards of behavior and identity? For James, this question can be answered two different ways. First, such ontological arrangements not only miss the point, but lead us away from an understanding of the richness of our capacities to engage with things. It is this very capacity that makes our worlds literally "engaging." He argued that we cannot and do not live within analytic systems, but that "what we need is practical reality, reality for ourselves; and, to have that, an object must not only appear, but it must appear both interesting and important."[19]

Second, James answered that pluralistic philosophical systems would not, do not, collapse without the imperatives of universalism. There is little possibility of solipsism, because only those who could abstract themselves from those things which surround them (that is, philosophers) could even imagine a radical disconnect between their selves and the things they use in everyday life. As James stated, "Whatever things have intimate and continuous connection with my life are things whose reality I cannot doubt."[20] Absolute skepticism can only be an hypothetical position.

Given, however, this constant stream of diverse experiential relationships with things, why do so many forms of Western philosophy decry them? And why do philosophy's approaches depend so heavily upon examples and conceptions of things while rejecting their centrality in the discovery and construction of truth? "But all philosophy *ends*," notes Jean-Luc Nancy, "by attributing (and while attributing) to the thing the thought that it elaborates about the thing."[21] To answer these questions, I turn to three intellectual periods in European history where the thing became central, though for different reasons in each: medieval Europe, the birth of modernity, and high modernity. As things become themselves—that is, as they cease to serve merely as representations of God's glory—their place within and outside of philosophy emerges. A quick sketch of the history of things' becoming (and the divergences intrinsic to those becomings) illuminates the role of things in thought.

### B. Three Places for Things

#### The Place of Things I: Display

Medieval Europe saw a tremendous explosion in things, which began to emerge as objects in their own right rather than expressions of a transcendent divine ordering. One locus of display materialized in the sixteenth century, a precursor to the later museum exhibitions of the modern: the *wunderkammern*. These "cabinets of wonder" ranged in size from cases that could be carried by hand to small rooms, but each had a similar purpose: the display of things that caused astonishment or fascination. The objects themselves were arranged not along modern taxonomical line, but displayed in juxtapositions intended to further arouse the viewer's interest.

Nor were the things' origins particularly differentiated. Oddities of nature such as exotic imports from distant lands (unicorn horns and ostrich eggs) and unusual indigenous objects (odd rocks and stuffed conjoined animals) were commingled with manmade wonders: miniature paintings, automata, or mathematical instruments. Additionally, the display structures themselves elicited amazement, not only as marvels of craftsmanship but also in sometimes possessing hidden drawers or recessed display areas.

One important aspect of these displays was the pleasure taken in their sensationalism. Traditional theology represented the wonders of the world as evidence of nature's (and therefore God's) economy and precision. But the *wunderkammern* "gloried in superfluity, careless of function and extravagant in expenditure of labor and materials."[22] A second noteworthy feature was the conflation between the natural and the manmade: discovered and created objects were shown together, simultaneous evidence of God's creation and of man's. Particular attention was paid to both those natural objects which appeared fabricated and those fabricated objects which imitated nature: *trompe l'oeil* and reproductions of animals in stone or bronze appeared next to shells which resembled gemstones or stones with naturally appearing images embedded within.[23]

Most important to the social history of things, however, was the degree to which it was distinctively understood that objects in and of themselves were deserving of attention. The purpose of the cabinet was to contain and display. Giorgio Agamben has argued that this moment comprises the creation of art itself, where the subjectivity of the artist (or artisan) diverges from the innermost "truth of consciousness" which art had heretofore served.[24] In other words, art and artifacts that serve God are merely fragments of a larger method of worship; art and artifacts that serve as *objects* in themselves divide the world of things and thus the world of men from the world of God.[25] The things within the cabinets no longer exist on the vertical axis of sacred meaning. When, in the transformative containment of the *wunderkammen*, things come into their own, ontological unity explodes.

### The Place of Things II: Doubt

By the middle of the seventeenth century, things were centered within logic and inquiry in European thought. That things were to be collected and displayed was by this time a truism. Wonderment and things were so closely aligned that Descartes could articulate in 1649 that "Wonder is the sudden surprise of the soul which makes it tend to consider attentively those *objects* which seem to it rare and extraordinary."[26] The notion that wonder is no longer reserved strictly (or even primarily) for God passes unremarked, a notable oddity in the work of someone dedicated to logically bolstering the existence of God.

For Descartes, as for his contemporaries Bacon and Pascal, epistemological truth had become bound up in things, things which by themselves cast as much doubt as certainty. Descartes's most famous suspicions of the world arose from those states of the sensation of things that, for individuals, had proven to be either wrong or uncertain: madness and dreaming. Descartes called into question the actuality of the surrounding world, primarily to try to find a nonphysical basis for proving his existence. Reality, for Descartes, must be founded outside the world of things.

And yet, this very testing of reality organizes itself around the material world. Descartes starts his meditative narratives by establishing the physical locale of the process: "I am here, sitting by the fire, wearing a winter dressing-gown, holding this piece of paper in my hands, and so on."[27] Through examples of his corporeal but doubtable existence, he moves to construct a rationality which ultimately can control the doubts and complications of the sensual world.[28]

Descartes never entirely escaped the realm of the thing. Even in the moment of the *cogito*, he identifies himself as "a thing that thinks."[29] The term "thing" is not meant to necessarily imply materiality or extension, of course, but nonetheless carries implications of tangibility. At another point, his extended allegorical treatment of wax takes up (surprisingly) more of the Second Meditation than does his self-identification as a thinking thing: four entire pages in the standard French edition of Descartes's writing.[30] "This piece of wax," Descartes argues, can be changed in infinite ways, being melted, reshaped, boiled, even frozen. Still, the wax remains the same wax regardless of its variation in shape, size, temperature, color, taste, texture, or sonorousness. Within the context of the meditations, the wax serves two exemplary functions in explaining a thing's identity: it identifies the truth of things with an essence not connected to their outward appearance, and it proves that true perception of a thing, even a corporeal thing, takes place with "the mind alone," not the senses.[31]

The oft-told philosophical narrative of Descartes's place in intellectual history suggests that he creates the modern subject through the process of rational thought.[32] But just as importantly, Descartes does so by positioning philosophy as extrinsic to objects, while simultaneously relying on their very thingness. The "thinking thing" can only be opposed to other "things"—things that still bear the taint of untrustworthiness—if one ignores that the same terminology is used for each. Things become what Descartes's philosophy builds itself against, while concurrently relying upon them for its very establishment.

## The Place of Things III: Limit

The modern philosophical conception of the thing reached its apotheosis with Kant. What Kant called the "thing in itself"—that is, the ultimate material nature of the object—formed both the basis for and the exteriority of logic and knowledge. Searching for the true grounds of philosophy, wherein one can distinguish the absolutely known from that which, like Descartes's object, remain questionable, Kant looked to *a priori* cognition, absolute thought which "occurs absolutely independently of all experience."[33]

Famously, Kant thereby defines things as the outer demarcation of what can therefore be known. The material world can never be comprehended by absolute knowledge. "Matter is *substania phaenomenon* [phenomenal substance]," he said, and as such "is not at all an object for pure understanding."[34] While we do certainly see, feel, and otherwise sense things, those sensations are merely sensations, and as such always outside the formal realm of reason. Appearances are not things in themselves; "things in themselves are entirely outside our sphere of cognition."[35] Hegel, Marx, and most of the nineteenth-century philosophers would follow Kant's trajectory in relegating things to the limit of philosophical thought (the complexities of the debates about the truth of the thing in itself are less important than its emergence as philosophy's center).

Among the most important Kantian reasons for this externality of things is the fact that things, in their sensate nature, can never be unified. That is, objects are always and irreducibly plural.

> But because every appearance contains a manifold, so that different perceptions are in themselves encountered in the mind sporadically and individually, these perceptions need to be given a combination that in sense themselves they cannot have.[36]

Kant's name for that combination: the human imagination. It is the imagination that depicts and orders empirical sensation through perception, a unity which does not exist within things in themselves. In other words, it is the mind, and only the mind, which brings objects together into unity.

Kantian philosophy therefore places things at the limit of human knowledge: They define the unknowable as well as provide the irreducible plurality of the world against which the mind constructs universality. As Heidegger put it, for Kant the "question 'What is a thing?' is the question 'Who is man?'"[37] One cannot be answered, or even asked, without the other.

## C. How to Do Words with Things

The Western philosophical tradition both disclaims things as what metaphysics must move beyond, and yet still relies upon things as the definition of this exteriority. So why this desire to exceed things? Why disclaim the very specificity, the specific discernments, of the world around us? Since Plato's parable of the Cave, the philosophical answer has been that the world of things distracts philosophy from truth, which exists in a world apart: the realm of Forms, or the City of God, or the truth of mathematical formulae.[38] In each variation, things lead away from and obscure truth, whereas logic, faith, and accuracy deliver it.

Yet this philosophical answer begs the question, for each version defines things as oppositional to truth while also defining truth as exclusively anti-material. An alternative way of answering this question—a Jamesian way—would be to find this desire to turn away from things as arising from psychological/social causes. The anti-materialist (in James's terms, the *idealist* or *spiritualist*) sees matter as "gross, coarse, crass, muddy; spirit is pure, elevated, noble; and since it is more consonant with the dignity of the universe to give the primacy in it to what appears superior, spirit must be affirmed as the ruling principle."[39] The desire for unity, faced with the obvious complexity and diversity of the world, demands a rejection of the world for the purity of unity.

Abstractions such as space, time, or the "thing-in-itself" are neither tangible nor actual, but are constructions with profound uses. At least, they are useful in certain limited circumstances; the spatial knowledge that a fire extinguisher is two feet away means very little unless one knows whether there is a locked door between it and the person who needs it. Certainly such abstractions do not reach the ideological pinnacle of universality for which they are invented. We live in spaces, not Space; through times, not Time; with things, not Things-in-themselves.

James's outlook on what matter itself does—and what is done with it—is an attempt to supersede these abstractions. Radical empiricism, not a materialism of abstract matter, makes things important. What things are and what is done with them are the same question, pragmatically speaking. For the "world of pure experience," it is the effect of a thing that holds sway, not its facticity or absolute existence. How things behave, in other words, is what things are. By extension, what other people do (that is, as things in their own right) is how we learn who they are: "it is only as altering my objects that I guess you to exist."[40]

And these behaviors of things, of necessity, are conjoined with us. Objects are altered, some alter themselves, and we in turn are changed. Things, in the words of Alphonso Lingis, "induce us to join our forces to theirs. Their forms are not simply shapes, boundaries, or contours; they are dynamic axes, concretizations of orientation."[41] Things and subjects, radical alterity and profound internality, all share connections and influences.

Given these overlaps, confluences, and interminglings, then, how can one make sense, even in a Jamesian way, of the plural engagements that necessarily follow? William James's initial answer, a limited one, is to focus strictly on the experiential aspects of existence, to follow the streams of consciousness that result from them. But experience, especially personal experience, too easily reduces to a unitary, ahistorical, and simplistic characterization.[42] Instead, there remain expansive and pluralistic answers to the questions to which philosophical pragmatics lead: What and where does it matter how we think of things?

**Philosophical Practices**

The last section of this chapter summarizes two ways of dealing with things, both radically pluralistic. The first, and more overtly practical, realms where the importance of thing-interactions take place are those still-developing theorizations of newly created and previously unknown practices. Changes in biological manipulations increasingly challenge previously unproblematic distinctions among the genetics of people, animals, and plants. Inventions in nanotechnology, microbial manipulation, and cybernetics further erase the ideal of a pure humanity, independent of the world of things.[43] One of the most thorough recent investigations of the relationships among the ontic, the ontological, and the pragmatic has come from recent attempts to theorize how objects should be represented in computational schematics.

Computers, of course, do not share a corporeal conception of objects—and how to relate programs to externalities constitutes a fundamental and pressing issue for those who create the codes by which computers function. Object-oriented system design is plagued not only by problems of categorization (How should a program count all things in a room? Is each speck of dust an object? What about a pile of sand?), but also by symbolic meaning-systems (Are blueprints objects? Are icons figures or labels? Are spatial relations figurative or literal?).

Brian Cantwell Smith's exploration of the philosophical issues involved in computational systems theory serves as a well-conceived, subtle introduction to these questions. In *On the Origin of Objects*, Smith connects problems of object-oriented system design with issues of past metaphysical contention.[44] He does not claim to solve theoretical issues per se (at least not beyond certain particular methodological problems), but in laying out the difficulties and some pragmatic solutions for conceptualizing objects, he eliminates the possibility that any unitary onticology could work.

For Smith, the simplistic conception of things wrongly serves both computers and philosophical systems. In multiple attempts to develop the programming capability to engage the physical world, the process of building a theoretical system of things and fitting computer programs into this organization proved fruitless. Ultimately, after many failures, those programmers attempting to address the treatment of things

> abandoned the idea that a system's ontological categories . . . should be explicitly represented at all. Instead, they viewed them emerging in constant and dynamic renegotiation with the environments in which these systems play or are explored.[45]

In other words, they developed a pluralistic outlook toward things. Smith uses the term *pluralism* repeatedly to describe the status of these ontic relationships. Rather than treating objects as either undifferentiated or unitary, their state should be expressed as shifting, circumstantial, and contextual. That is, each thing exists not as a singular Object, but as a range of objectival possibilities, likelihoods, uses, and engagements. To use Bergson's term, it is "degrees in spatiality," not things, with which computers must engage.[46]

Smith makes clear that such a pluralism is not the formalized pluralism of mid-twentieth-century political science (or even of contemporary multiculturalism). Conceiving of resolutely isolated "ways of thinking" (whether individual, cultural, or regional) as intrinsically and irreducibly different, Smith argues, cuts off the very ability to interact across identities, to contest one another, and to share the experience of objects. Such an approach does "not even extend to outsiders the respect of allowing them to be wrong."[47] The pluralism which objects demand of computational systems denies the possibility of absolute and ecumenical representation—it leaves open the potentiality of objects. This, above all, is a Jamesian pluralism.

## Practical Philosophies

The second way of making sense of our theoretical pragmatics of objects entails the possibility of an overt reversal of the relationship of things to ideas. What if philosophy does not exceed things, but instead grows out of attempts to grapple with things, to "put them in their place"? Recall the triptych of historical places for things at the center of this chapter: each serves as an attempt to decide the proper place for things in each particular era.

Why should philosophical exploration take as its goal inquiry into truth as distinct from the material world? Indeed, why should the causal relation be so commonly seen as that of theory over matter, of philosophy above things? From a strictly or implicitly theological orientation this ordering makes sense: there must be a creator before a creation, whether in the Judaic book of Genesis or in Timaeus's monologue to Socrates.[48] But philosophically, such assumed directionality should be suspect; indeed, any individual person's growth and progression from infancy involves at least as much engagement with things as with overt ontological foundationalist philosophy.

For James, the most suspect and "Hegelian" tradition in philosophical thinking is the tendency to lump all questions, experiences, and ideas into an allegedly unified system, dismissing and discounting all that does not fit. Generally, even if called "materialism," such a system purports to reach the real truth behind the things, such as Marx's contention that social relations, in determining the means of production, create things that are irrevocably and individually accounted for by the socioeconomic system that made them.

This reductionism not only does violence to the variety of uses and meanings that things can have, but is also theoretically incoherent. Alec McHoul has noted that objects need to register in multiple dimensions in order to be meaningful at all: If a thing were ever a "hypothetically pure" object, it would be impenetrable to human understanding.[49] James makes a similar point in criticizing this absolutism:

> When we speak of the absolute we take the one universal known material collectively or integrally; when we speak of its objects . . . we take that same identical material distributively and separately. But what is the use of a thing's *being* only once if it can be taken twice over, and if *being* taken in different ways makes different things true of it?[50]

In this, James's better-known pragmatism and his pluralism coalesce. We do multiple things with things, in multiple ways: to insist on their unitarity would be to misunderstand our relationships with them. That truths can be multiple, partial, or conditional in order to be useful is no more contentious than to say the same of things. We come to the world already engaged with it, making what we can and what we will of its multitudes. Philosophical thinking, for James, means making sense of these diverse encounters—and not eliminating them one by one, leaving only a nonmaterial absolutism.

Writing, argued Italo Calvino, should not be for discovering or deciphering "the only reality we can know, indeed the only reality *tout court*," but that we should instead use "words as a perpetual pursuit of things, as a perpetual adjustment to their infinite variety."[51] In this understanding, as in James's, we do not merely adjust things, we adjust ourselves to them. In doing so, we continue to participate in, even embrace, the vast multiplicity of which our worlds consist.

## Notes

1. Marcel Mauss, *The Gift: The Form and Reason for Exchange in Archaic Societies*, trans. W. D. Halls (New York: W. W. Norton, 1990), p. 49.

2. John Elof Boodin, "William James as I Knew Him," *William James Remembered*, ed. Linda Simon (Lincoln: University of Nebraska Press, 1996), pp. 207–39, quotation on pp. 221–22.

3. Though he does not use this specific example, Kim Townsend adeptly articulates the implicit form of masculinist discourse in U.S. academia of the time; see his *Manhood at Harvard: William James and Others* (New York: W. W. Norton, 1996).

4. William James, *Pragmatism and the Meaning of Truth* (Cambridge, MA: Harvard University Press, 1978), pp. 90–91.

5. "All things have tears."

6. I address the politics of this relationship in *The Politics of Judgment: Aesthetics, Identity, and Political Theory* (Lanham, MD: Lexington Books, 1999).

7. Elaine Scarry, *The Body in Pain: The Making and Unmaking of the World* (Oxford, UK: Oxford University Press, 1985), p. 53.

8. Cf. Arjun Appadurai, *The Social Life of Things: Commodities in Cultural Perspective*, (Cambridge, UK: Cambridge University Press, 1986).

9. James, *Pragmatism*, pp. 85–86.

10. James, *Pragmatism*, p. 209.

11. Karl Marx and Frederick Engels, "The Holy Family, or Critique of Critical Criticism: Against Bruno Bauer and Company," *Collected Works, vol. 4 (1844–1845)*, trans. Richard Dixon and Clemens Dutt (London: Lawrence & Wishart, 1975), pp. 8–211 (see esp. pp. 124–43).

12. Marx and Engels, "The Holy Family," p. 130.

13. William James, *The Varieties of Religious Experience* (New York: Mentor, 1958), p. 404.

14. Ralph Barton Perry, *In the Spirit of William James* (Bloomington: Indiana University Press, 1958), p. 119.

15. *APU*, p. 117.

16. William James, *The Principles of Psychology*, vol. II, (Cambridge, MA: Harvard University Press, 1981), pp. 722–75.

17. James, *Principles*, vol. II, pp. 1253–62; see also p. 657.

18. James M. Edie, *William James and Phenomenology* (Bloomington: Indiana University Press, 1987), pp. 2–3.

19. James, *Principles*, vol. II, p. 295.

20. James, *Principles*, vol. II, p. 298.

21. Jean-Luc Nancy, *The Birth to Presence*, trans. Brian Holmes (Stanford, CA: Stanford University Press, 1993), p. 179 (emphasis in original).

22. Lorraine Daston and Katharine Park, *Wonders and the Order of Nature 1150–1750* (New York: Zone Books, 1998), p. 277.

23. Daston and Park find this conflation between art and nature to be the overarching appeal of such cabinets, but many *wunderkammern* did not juxtapose the artificial and the natural, and some contained only constructed objects.

24. Giorgio Agamben, *The Man Without Content*, trans. Georgia Albert (Stanford, CA: Stanford University Press, 1999), p. 33.

25. This disjuncture is most forcefully noted by Hegel, in his *Aesthetics* (volumes 1 and 2, trans. T. M. Knox [Oxford, UK: Oxford University Press, 1975]). But for Hegel (and consequently for Agamben), it is art which leaves the realm of the sacred; for my purposes the effect here on the material world has far more import.

26. René Descartes, *The Passions of the Soul*, trans. Stephen Voss (Indianapolis: Hackett, 1989), p. 56 (italics mine).

27. René Descartes, *The Philosophical Writings of Descartes*, vol. II, trans. John Cottingham, Robert Stoothoff, and Dugald Murdoch (Cambridge, UK: Cambridge University Press, 1984), p. 13.

28. Michel Foucault points out that Descartes here partakes in both the logical construction of a syllogistic structure and also the enactment of a narrative of meditation, the latter evoking and inviting participation by the reader in a destabilizing process. Foucault calls the former a "system," the latter an "exercise." One could easily note that the former works to exclude things from reality, while the latter entrenches things' centrality. "My Body, This Paper, This Fire," in *Aesthetics, Method, and Epistemology: Essential Works of Foucault*, Volume II, ed. James D. Faubion, trans. Geoff Bennington (New York: The New Press, 1998), pp. 393–417.

29. Descartes, *Philosophical Writings*, vol. II, p. 18.

30. *Oeuvres de Descartes*, ed. Charles Adam and Paul Tannery (Paris: Cerf, 1896).

31. Descartes, *Philosophical Writings*, vol. II, p. 21.

32. Matthew L. Jones shows how the complexity of the role of mathematics in Descartes's thought undermines this story of intentionality. He also points out that Descartes must overtly construct mathematics as a unitary "thing" in order to use it as a foundation for cognition. See his "Descartes's Geometry as Spiritual Exercise" in *Critical Inquiry* 28, no. 1 (Autumn 2001), pp. 40–71, esp. p. 63.

33. Immanuel Kant, *Critique of Pure Reason, Unified Edition*, trans. Werner S. Pluhar (Indianapolis: Hackett, 1996), p. 3. (Unless otherwise designated, page references are to the 1787 German second edition.)

34. Kant, *Critique of Pure Reason*, p. 333.

35. Kant, *Critique of Pure Reason*, p. 235.

36. Kant, *Critique of Pure Reason*, section III of the first edition, p. 120.

37. Martin Heidegger, *What Is a Thing?* trans. W. B. Barton and Vera Deutsch (Chicago: Henry Regnery, 1967), p. 244.

38. Hannah Arendt, in *Between Past and Future* (New York: Penguin, 1977), suggests that the world Plato rejects is that of action. But the parable itself and the dialogues in general strongly suggest that it is objects, not actions, which tempt us in our misconceptions.

39. William James, *Pragmatism*, 50. It is worth noting here, however, that James is merely agreeing with Spencer about this particular point, that such a conception is ridiculous. Ultimately, he holds at this point the distinction that matter and God are equally useful, in the sense that each makes a claim about origination that has little to do with the effects and engagements with the material world, whatever its foundation.

40. William James, *Essays in Radical Empiricism* (Cambridge, MA: Harvard University Press, 1976), p. 39.

41. Alphonso Lingis, *The Imperative* (Bloomington: Indiana University Press, 1998), pp. 82–83.

42. Joan W. Scott, "Experience," *Feminists Theorize the Political*, ed. Judith Butler and Joan W. Scott (New York: Routledge, 1992).

43. Donna Haraway, "A Manifesto for Cyborgs: Science, Technology and Socialist Feminism in the 1980s," *Socialist Review* 80, pp. 65–108; Jane Bennett, *The Enchantment of Modern Life: Attachments, Crossing, and Ethics* (Princeton, NJ: Princeton University Press, 2001).

44. Brian Cantwell Smith, *On the Origin of Objects* (Cambridge, MA: MIT Press, 1996).

45. Smith, *On the Origin of Objects*, p. 48.

46. Henri Bergson, *Creative Evolution*, trans. Arthur Mitchell (New York: Henry Holt and Co., 1911), p. 250. See also his critique of Kantian space, pp. 203–6.

47. Bergson, *Creative Evolution*, p. 113.

48. See, for example, John Sallis, *Chorology: On Beginning in Plato's Timaeus* (Bloomington: Indiana University Press, 1999). See also Charles E. Scott's gloss on this in *The Lives of Things* (Bloomington: Indiana University Press, 2002), pp. 36–50.

49. Alec McHoul, "Ordinary Heterodoxies: Toward a Theory of Cultural Objects," *UTS Review* 8, no. 3. (1997), pp. 7–22.

50. William James, *A Pluralistic Universe* (Cambridge, MA: Harvard University Press, 1977), p. 22 (emphasis in original).

51. Italo Calvino, *Six Memos for the New Millenium (The Charles Eliot Norton Lectures, 1985–1986)*, (Cambridge, MA: Harvard University Press, 1988), p. 26.

# Conclusion

THE MODERN WORLD SUFFERS AGORAPHOBIA, argues Rosalyn Deutsche.[1] Like other forms, this particular agoraphobia is the fear of wide-open spaces, but these specific spaces are conceptual in nature. The plurality of the world, the reluctance of those most different from us to play by our rules, and the open-ended nature of the future all threaten our stability and predictability. Drawing on the critical analyses of Claude Lefort, Iris Marion Young, and Thomas Keenan, Deutsche describes various attempts to reclaim the allegedly lost history of public space in the name of a vanished, threatened, and universal "public" which only exists in the nostalgic imaginary.

Thus, nostalgia serves as the conceptual safe house for modern agoraphobics.[2] (Like other safe houses, it is difficult both to get into and to escape from.) To the nostalgic, the political and social world of the past constituted a stable and solid realm of commonality, where contestation was circumspect, politics genteel, and acrimony fleeting. In this past, those on the wrong teleological side of history would eventually realize their errors, most of which would then become superfluous. Thus, in the United States, those who held contrary conceptions of America's past (for example, the Native Americans who argued that the land was theirs, or the robber barons who took advantage of poor workers, or the communists and hippies who sought revolution) never truly threatened the great consensus of history. They never won and, as viewed from the present, never could have.

The present, on the other hand, presents a greater peril. Dangerous, uncooperative, and immoral people threaten the very essence of the political world, precisely because they have the potential to change things. The specters of

Mexican immigrants, religious extremists, and gay activists seem unprecedented, for they could actually alter the existing social and political makeup of the country. Thus, the agoraphobic constantly refers back to the safety of the past, where such menacing possibilities could never really materialize.

William James, in this conception, was an agoraphile. Pluralism dooms the simplifying nostrums of nostalgia. Nostalgic history, in its relative fixities, lacks potentiality. We change; history remains. For James, the possibilities of the future took precedence over the artificial certainties of nostalgia. Agoraphilia, in other words, is the opening of the self to the variety of engagements it encounters. It embraces the potential of those engagements, even those which threaten its apparently rock-solid commitments. (One could ask the nostalgic: If you are so steadfast, why are you so easily threatened?) Life's multiplicity and variety constitute opportunities as much as threats and they are the latter only when the self and the community are fixed and certain.

This is not to reject the past, of course. For pluralists, history instead blooms with unfollowed potentialities and overflows with secret alternatives. The flowering of Foucaultian historiography, for example, views the past as filled with archaeological sites of alternatives. Instead of the story of how a people came to be, such approaches to history emphasize what was lost and what roads remain untaken. Treating history pluralistically means attending to the genealogical alternatives buried within the sedimentation of its universalizing narrative.

One historical question was as common in James's time as in our own: What does the United States stand for? The common reading tells a two-century story of gradually expanding rights for all individuals, helped along by the salutary confluence of capitalism and democracy. To that telling stands a number of threats—immigrants unappreciative of our values, terrorists despising our freedoms, nattering nabobs of negativism devaluing our achievements.

In James's era, of course, the United States stood for the same things and thus was menaced by the same threats. James had to argue to admit students of African ancestry into his own university. He fought against lynching, seen as merely an unfortunate excess of Southern self-rule. He argued against imperialists, who were determined to improve inferior peoples by force, and against isolationists, who demanded protection from the same inferior peoples. He stood for free speech, free thought, and free individuals.

Today, the popular story of American exceptionalism positions civil rights as the inevitable outcome of a political democracy. This story effectively ignores and insults those activists who created its conditions and made it happen—they merely serve as menservants (and womenservants) to history. If civil rights were foreordained, then the sacrifices and articulations of Frederick Douglass, Sojourner Truth, Ida B. Wells, W. E. B. DuBois, Martin Luther King Jr., and the thousands of people who stood alongside them are meaningless, since the same results would have eventually appeared regardless of those people's efforts. If, on the other hand, this history was fragile, contested, particular, and hard-fought, if each era contained multiple possibilities and potentialities, if it was, in a word, *plural*—then these individuals and their ideas were truly courageous and influential. We can debate their heroism only insofar as no teleological necessity exists.

The majority of Americans considered these civil rights leaders to be a threat. They stood for positions emphatically antithetical to those of most U.S. citizens, and their inspiration and willingness threatened the "consensual" views of America and democracy. One lesson to take from this may be that of heroism, in which we learn to evaluate and examine our own time, looking for those among us who find inspiration in such leaders. But another, less common lesson may be to examine the assumptions and criticisms of the Americans who opposed them, and note where we internalize and parrot the same analyses. Rather than solidifying the past into a hardened chronicle, we can use histories to interrogate our own certainties.

Where do I fear difference? Who do I wish to exclude from the boundaries of the social or political, and what conceptual delimitations do I employ to enforce these expulsions? What norms and naturalisms do I replicate, and how do those serve to disenfranchise and exclude? These are the questions encouraged by a pluralist reading of history, whether of civil rights, other political rights (like women's suffrage, worker's rights, and other parallel historical themes), or social/political/ethical transformations of any sort, from any time or place.

William James was not a historian, but a psychologist and a philosopher. The uncertainties and multiplicities of psychology in a post-Freudian age have become relatively comprehensible: The idea that aspects of the human psyche will remain unexplained bothers few today. But philosophy presents a different matter—the idealism of a universality of truth persists, and pluralism and pragmatism's challenges to it still invite controversy.

This is especially apparent within political theory. The settlement of issues has long comprised the motivating purview of political philosophy. The logical treatment of politics, after all, has promised to bring a stage of optimized decisions, predictable populations, and achievable consensus. Political science, in other words, has been posited as a set of solutions for an agoraphobic world.

If Jamesian pluralism has an ethos, then, it opposes this conception of politics. Politics, in a prescriptively pluralistic sense, should be about opening contested spaces rather than closing them off: noting the locations of exclusion, encouraging disavowal and dissent, and subverting consensus. This resembles modern conceptions of art more than classical conceptions of science. Political creation and progress in politics do not build a sound, stable edifice; they proliferate new spaces and differing possibilities.

Of course, this requires a concomitant rethinking of politics and political action. Rather than establishing general agreement, politics would become a seedbed of dissension. Political actors could see themselves as creating concepts, motivations, and new sensibilities. These should emerge both in concert with and in opposition to the multiple points of agreement and disagreement already extant in political and social culture.

Above all, such a political pluralism challenges the orthodox. Attempting to fix things to an absolutist meaning, whether ideological or material, leads to the intrinsic contradiction of orthodoxy. Orthodoxy, as such, cannot truly exist, though it can be, and often is, defended to the death. As Michel de Certeau points out, orthodoxy is the promise of truth and of singularity. But in making such a promise (that no other interpretations, no different uses of things, can exist), any orthodoxy necessarily invites its negation, by suggesting the likelihood of alternative interpretations and uses. By definition, orthodoxy creates the very conditions of heterodoxy.[3]

What kinds of philosophy can remain, then, without the sureties of universalism? Philosophies that take their terms from the world's creations and profusions, rather than by attempting to force a sterile universe to conform, could be called theories of *heterodox materialism*. Such approaches need not reach the same conclusions, nor must they provide moral systems that demand beliefs or actions. Heterodox materialisms, while closely linked to pluralist philosophies, need not necessarily lead to any specific orientation. The possibilities of such attitudes are absent from the great systemetizers; Plato, Locke, Kant, and Hegel each attempted to construct orthodoxies, systems of logic which compel assent. Instead, those who investigate, contemplate, and to some extent embrace the role of things in our lives could, conceivably, animate pluralistic outlooks.[4] These would look more like the theoretical outsiders in the philosophic tradition. The philosophies of Liebniz, for whom all things reflect and ultimately contain all other things. The philosophies of Spinoza, for whom only the concept of infinite variation can make existence possible. The philosophies of Bergson, for whom logics pale in comparison to the constant changes and the discontinuities comprising the eternal present in which each human lives. And, of course, the philosophies of William James, who warns against those looking to intellectual inquiry for reasons to ignore, exclude, and deprecate those things and people and ideas that populate our rich and manifold worlds.

## Notes

1. Rosalyn Deutsche, *Evictions: Art and Spatial Politics* (Cambridge, MA: MIT Press, 1996), pp. 269–327.
2. Wendy Hui Kyong Chun spells out the connections between agoraphobia and nostalgia in *Control and Freedom: Power and Paranoia in the Age of Fiber Optics* (Cambridge, MA: MIT Press, 2006), pp. 247–50.
3. Michel de Certeau, "Is There a Language of Unity?" trans. Lancelot Sheppard, *Concilium* 51 (1970), 79–93.
4. One could even take this call to animation literally. See Jane Bennett, "The Force of Things: Steps Toward an Ecology of Matter," *Political Theory* 32, no. 3, pp. 347–72.

# Bibliography

Agamben, Giorgio. *The Man without Content*, trans. Georgia Albert. Stanford, CA: Stanford University Press, 1999.

Antliff, Mark. *Inventing Bergson: Cultural Politics and the Parisian Avant-Garde*. Princeton, NJ: Princeton University Press, 1993.

Appadurai, Arjun. *The Social Life of Things: Commodities in Cultural Perspective*. Cambridge, UK: Cambridge University Press, 1986.

Arendt, Hannah. *Between Past and Future*. New York: Penguin, 1977.

———. "Reflections on Little Rock." In *Responsibility and Judgment*, ed. Jerome Kohn. New York: Shocken Books, 2003, 193–213.

Ashley, Richard. "Living on Border Lines: Man, Post-Structuralism, and War." In *International/Intertextual Relations*, ed. James Der Derian and Michael Shapiro. New York: Lexington Books, 1989, 259–321.

———. "Untying the Sovereign State: A Double Reading of the Anarchy Problematique." *Millennium* 17 (1988): 227–63.

Ashley, Richard K., and R. B. J. Walker. "Reading Dissidence/Writing the Discipline: Crisis and the Question of Sovereignty in International Studies." *International Studies Quarterly* 34: 367–416.

Ayer, A. J. *The Origins of Pragmatism: Studies in the Philosophy of Charles Sanders Pierce and William James*. London: MacMillan, 1968.

Barber, Benjamin R. *Jihad vs. McWorld*. New York: Times Books, 1995.

Bartleson, Jens. *A Genealogy of Sovereignty*. Cambridge, UK: Cambridge University Press, 1995.

Beisner, Robert. *Twelve Against Empire: The Anti-Imperialists 1898–1900*. New York: McGraw-Hill, 1968.

Benhabib, Seyla, Judith Butler, Drucilla Cornell, and Nancy Fraser. *Feminist Contentions: A Philosophical Exchange*. New York: Routledge, 1995.

Bennett, Jane. *The Enchantment of Modern Life: Attachments, Crossing, and Ethics.* Princeton, NJ: Princeton University Press, 2001.

———. "The Force of Things: Steps toward an Ecology of Matter." *Political Theory* 32 (2004): 347–72.

Bergson, Henri. *Creative Evolution*, trans. Arthur Mitchell. New York: Henry Holt and Co., 1911.

———. *Key Writings*, ed. Keith Ansell Pearson and John Mullarkey. New York: Continuum, 2002.

———. *Introduction to Metaphysics*, trans. Mabelle L. Andison. New York: Wisdom Library, 1961.

———. *Matter and Memory*, trans. Nancy Margaret Paul and W. Scott Palmer. London: Allen and Unwin, 1911.

———. *Mélanges*. Paris: Presses Universitaires de France, 1972.

———. *The Two Sources of Morality and Religion*, trans. R. Ashely Audra and Cloudesley Brereton. New York: Henry Holt, 1935.

Berlin, Isaiah. *Against the Current: Essays in the History of Ideas*, ed. Henry Hardy. New York: Viking, 1980.

———. *Four Essays on Liberty.* New York: Oxford University Press, 1969.

———. *The Roots of Romanticism*, ed. Henry Hardy. Princeton, NJ: Princeton University Press, 1999.

———. *Vico and Herder: Two Studies in the History of Ideas.* London: Hogarth Press, 1976.

Bohman, James. "The Moral Costs of Political Pluralism." In *Hannah Arendt: Twenty Years Later*, ed. Larry May and Jerome Kohn. Cambridge, MA: MIT Press, 1996, 53–80.

Boodin, John Elof. "William James as I Knew Him," In *William James Remembered*, ed. Linda Simon. Lincoln: University of Nebraska Press, 1996, 207–39.

Boutroux, Emile. *William James.* New York: Longman's, Green, 1912.

Butler, Christopher. *Early Modernism: Literature, Music and Painting in Europe, 1900–1916.* Oxford, UK: Oxford University Press, 1994.

Calvino, Italo. *Six Memos for the New Millennium (The Charles Eliot Norton Lectures, 1985–1986).* Cambridge, MA: Harvard University Press, 1988, 26.

Campbell, David. *National Deconstruction: Violence, Identity, and Justice in Bosnia.* Minneapolis: University of Minnesota Press, 1998.

———. *Writing Security: United States Foreign Policy and the Politics of Identity.* Minneapolis: University of Minnesota Press, 1992.

Čapek, Milič. *Bergson and Modern Physics: A Reinterpretation and Re-evaluation.* Dordrect: Reidel, 1971.

Certeau, Michel de. "Is There a Language of Unity?" trans. Lancelot Sheppard. *Concilium* 51 (1970): 79–93.

Chun, Wendy Hui Kyong. *Control and Freedom: Power and Paranoia in the Age of Fiber Optics.* Cambridge, MA: MIT Press, 2006.

Cole, G. D. H. *Guild Socialism Restated.* London: L. Parsons, 1920.

———. *The Social Theory.* London: Methuen and Co., 1920.

Colletti, Lucio. *Marxism and Hegel*, trans. Lawrence Garner. London: Verso, 1979.

Connolly, William, ed. *The Bias of Pluralism.* New York: Atherton Press, 1969.
——. *The Ethos of Pluralization.* Minneapolis: University of Minnesota Press, 1995.
——. *Pluralism.* Durham, NC: Duke University Press, 2005.
Cotkin, George. *William James, Public Philosopher.* Urbana: University of Illinois Press, 1989.
Crowder, George. *Liberalism and Value Pluralism.* London: Continuum, 2002.
Culler, Jonathan, and Brian Lamb, eds. *Just Being Difficult? Academic Writing in the Public Arena.* Stanford, CA: Stanford University Press, 2003.
Cusimano, Maryann K. *Beyond Sovereignty: Issues for a Global Agenda.* New York: Bedford, 2000.
Dahl, Robert. *Dilemmas of Pluralist Democracy: Autonomy vs. Control.* New Haven, CT: Yale University Press, 1982.
——. *Pluralistic Democracy in the United States.* Chicago: Rand McNally & Co, 1967.
——. *A Preface to Democratic Theory.* Chicago: University of Chicago Press, 1956.
Daston, Lorraine, and Katharine Park. *Wonders and the Order of Nature, 1150–1750.* New York: Zone Books, 1998.
Deleuze, Gilles. *Bergsonism,* trans. Hugh Tomlinson and Barbara Habberjam. New York: Zone Books, 1988.
——. *Cinema 1: The Movement-Image,* trans. Hugh Tomlinson and Barbara Habberjam. London: Athlone, 1986.
——. *Cinema 2: The Time-Image,* trans. Hugh Tomlinson and Robert Galeta. London: Athlone, 1988.
Deleuze, Gilles, and Félix Guattari. *A Thousand Plateaus: Capitalism and Schizophrenia,* trans. Brian Massumi. Minneapolis: University of Minnesota Press, 1987.
Deleuze, Gilles, and Claire Parnet. *Dialogues,* trans. Hugh Tomlinson and Barbara Hammerjam. London: Althone, 1987.
Denham, Mark, and Mark Owen Lombardi, eds. *Perspectives on Third-World Sovereignty: The Postmodern Paradox.* London: MacMillan Press Ltd., 1996.
Der Derian, James. *On Diplomacy: A Genealogy of Western Estrangement.* New York: Basil Blackwell, 1987.
Descartes, René. *Oeuvres de Descartes,* ed. Charles Adam and Paul Tannery. Paris: Cerf, 1896.
——. *The Passions of the Soul,* trans. Stephen Voss. Indianapolis: Hackett, 1989.
——. *The Philosophical Writings of Descartes,* trans. John Cottingham, Robert Stoothoff, and Dugald Murdoch. Cambridge, UK: Cambridge University Press, 1984.
Deutsche, Rosalyn. *Evictions: Art and Spatial Politics.* Cambridge, MA: The MIT Press, 1996.
Dewey, John. *The Middle Works, 1899–1924,* ed. Jo Ann Boydston. Carbondale: Southern Illinois University Press, 1976–1983.
——. *The Public and Its Problems.* New York: Henry Holt and Co., 1927.
Doty, Roxanne Lynn. *Imperial Encounters: The Politics of Representation in North-South Relations.* Minneapolis: University of Minnesota Press, 1996.
Duguit, Léon. *Law in the Modern State.* New York: Viking Press, 1919.
Dumm, Thomas L. *Michel Foucault and the Politics of Freedom.* Thousand Oaks, CA: Sage Publications, 1996.

Durkheim, Emile. *Pragmatism and Sociology*, trans. J. C. Whitehouse. Cambridge, UK: Cambridge University Press, 1983.

Edie, James M. *William James and Phenomenology*. Bloomington: Indiana University Press, 1987.

Eisenberg, Avigail. *Reconstructing Political Pluralism*. Albany: State University of New York Press, 1995.

Enloe, Cynthia. *Bananas, Beaches and Bases: Making Feminist Sense of World Politics*. Berkeley: University of California Press, 2001.

Faulkner, William. *William Faulkner: Novels 1942–1954: Go Down, Moses / Intruder in the Dust / Requiem for a Nun / A Fable*. New York: Library of America, 1994.

Ferguson, Kennan. "I ♥ My Dog." *Political Theory* 32 (2004): 373–95.

———. *The Politics of Judgment: Aesthetics, Identity, and Political Theory*. Lanham, MD: Lexington Books, 1999.

Figgis, J. N. *Churches in the Modern State*. London: Longmans, 1914.

Flathman, Richard. *Willful Liberalism: Voluntarism and Individuality in Theory and Practice*. Ithaca, NY: Cornell University Press, 1992.

Flournoy, Théodore. *The Philosophy of William James*, trans. Edwin B. Holt and William James Jr. London: Constable & Company, 1917.

Foucault, Michel. "My Body, This Paper, This Fire." In *Aesthetics, Method, and Epistemology: Essential Works of Foucault Volume II*, ed. James D. Faubion, trans. Geoff Bennington. New York: The New Press, 1998, 393–417.

———. *The Foucault Effect: Studies in Governmentality*, ed. Graham Burchell, Colin Gordon, and Peter Miller. Chicago: University of Chicago Press, 1991.

Gray, John. *Isaiah Berlin*. Princeton, NJ: Princeton University Press, 1996.

———. *Two Faces of Liberalism*. New York: The New Press, 2000.

Grossman, Joan Delany. "Philosophers, Decadents, and Mystics: James's Russian Readers in the 1890s." In *William James and Russian Culture*, ed. Joan Delany Grossman and Ruth Rischin. Lanham, MD: Lexington, 2003, 93–111.

Haraway, Donna. "A Manifesto for Cyborgs: Science, Technology and Socialist Feminism in the 1980s." *Socialist Review* 80 (1985), 65–108.

Hardt, Michael, and Antonio Negri, *Empire*. Cambridge, MA: Harvard University Press, 2000.

———. *Multitude: War and Democracy in the Age of Empire*. London; Penguin, 2004.

Hass, Ernst B. *Nationalism, Liberalism, and Progress*. Ithaca, NY: Cornell University Press, 1997.

Hegel, Georg Wilhelm Friedrich. *Aesthetics, I & II*, trans. T. M. Knox. Oxford, UK: Oxford University Press, 1975.

Heidegger, Martin. *What Is a Thing?*, trans. W. B. Barton and Vera Deutsch. Chicago: Henry Regnery, 1967.

Hinsley, F. H. *Sovereignty*. Cambridge, UK: Cambridge University Press, 1986.

Holmes, Oliver Wendell, Jr., and Harold J. Laski. *Holmes-Laski Letters: The Correspondence of Mr. Justice Holmes and Harold J. Laski, 1916–1935*, Vol. 1, ed. Mark De Wolfe Howe. Cambridge, MA: Harvard University Press, 1953.

Honig, Bonnie. *Political Theory and the Displacement of Politics*. Ithaca, NY: Cornell University Press, 1993.

Hsiao, Kung Chuan. *Political Pluralism: A Study in Contemporary Political Theory.* New York: Harcourt, Brace & Company, 1927.
Huntington, Samuel. *The Clash of Civilizations and the Remaking of World Order.* New York: Simon & Schuster, 1998.
———. *Who We Are: The Challenges to America's National Identity.* New York: Simon & Schuster, 2004.
James, William. *Essays, Comments, and Reviews.* Cambridge, MA: Harvard University Press, 1987.
———. *Essays in Philosophy.* Cambridge, MA: Harvard University Press, 1978.
———. *Essays in Psychology.* Cambridge, MA: Harvard University Press, 1983.
———. *Essays in Radical Empiricism.* Cambridge, MA: Harvard University Press, 1976.
———. *Essays in Religion and Morality.* Cambridge, MA: Harvard University Press, 1982.
———. *Letters of William James,* ed. Henry James. Boston: Atlantic Monthly Press, 1920.
———. *The Meaning of Truth.* Cambridge, MA: Harvard University Press, 1975.
———. *A Pluralistic Universe.* Cambridge, MA: Harvard University Press, 1975.
———. *Pragmatism.* Cambridge, MA: Harvard University Press, 1975.
———. *Pragmatism and the Meaning of Truth.* Cambridge, MA: Harvard University Press, 1978.
———. *Principles of Psychology, I & II.* Cambridge, MA: Harvard University Press, 1981.
———. *Talks to Teachers on Psychology and to Students on Some of Life's Ideals.* Cambridge, MA: Harvard University Press, 1983.
———. *The Varieties of Religious Experience.* Cambridge, MA: Harvard University Press, 1985.
———. *Writings, 1902–1910.* New York: Library of America, 1988.
James, William, and Théodore Flournoy. *The Letters of William James and Theodore Flournoy,* ed. Robert C. Le Clair. Madison: University of Wisconsin Press, 1999.
Johnston, Steven. *Encountering Tragedy: Rousseau and the Project of Democratic Order.* Ithaca, NY: Cornell University Press, 1999.
Jones, Matthew L. "Descartes's Geometry as Spiritual Exercise." *Critical Inquiry* 28 (2001), 40–71.
Joyce, James. *Finnegans Wake.* London: Penguin, 1976.
Kallen, Horace. *William James and Henri Bergson: A Study in Contrasting Theories of Life.* Chicago: University of Chicago Press, 1914.
Kant, Immanuel. *Critique of Pure Reason, Unified Edition,* trans. Werner S. Pluhar. Indianapolis: Hackett, 1996.
Kariel, Henry S. *The Decline of American Pluralism.* Stanford, CA: Stanford University Press, 1961.
Kaufman-Osborn, Timothy V. "John Dewey and the Liberal Science of Community." *The Journal of Politics* 46 (1984): 1142–65.
Keohane, Robert O. *After Hegemony: Cooperation and Discord in the World Political Economy.* Princeton, NJ: Princeton University Press, 1984.
Keohane, Robert O., and Joseph Nye, eds. *Transnational Relations and World Politics.* Cambridge, MA: Harvard University Press, 1972.

Kimball, Roger. *Tenured Radicals: How Politics Has Corrupted Our Higher Education.* New York: HarperCollins, 1990.
Kocis, Robert. *A Critical Appraisal of Sir Isaiah Berlin's Political Philosophy.* Lewiston, NY: The Edward Mellen Press, 1989.
Krasner, Stephen D. *Sovereignty: Organized Hypocrisy.* Princeton, NJ: Princeton University Press, 2001.
Laski, Harold J. *Authority in the Modern State.* New Haven, CT: Yale University Press, 1919.
———. *The Foundations of Sovereignty and Other Essays.* New York: Harcourt, Brace, 1921.
———. *A Grammar of Politics.* New Haven, CT: Yale University Press, 1925.
———. *Liberty in the Modern State.* New York: Viking Press, 1949.
———. "Political Pluralism." *The New Republic* 54 (1928): 197.
———. *Studies in Law and Politics.* New Haven, CT: Yale University Press, 1932.
———. *Studies in the Problem of Sovereignty.* New York: Howard Fertig, 1968.
Lenin, V. I. *Materialism and Empiriocriticism,* trans. Abraham Fineburg. Moscow: Progress Publishers, 1972.
Lentricchia, Frank. "The Return of William James." *Cultural Critique* 4 (1986): 5–31.
Levinas, Emmanuel. *Time and the Other,* trans. Richard A. Cohen. Pittsburgh: Duquesne University Press, 1987.
Lingis, Alphonso. *The Imperative.* Bloomington: Indiana University Press, 1998.
MacIver, Robert. *The Web of Government.* New York: MacMillan Company, 1947.
Mackenzie, W. J. M. "Representation in Plural Societies." *Political Studies* 2 (1954): 54–69.
Macpherson, C. B. *Democratic Theory: Essays in Retrieval.* Oxford, UK: Clarendon Press, 1973.
Magid, Henry Meyer. *English Political Pluralism: The Problem of Freedom and Organization.* New York: Columbia University Press, 1941.
Manganiello, Dominic. *Joyce's Politics.* London: Routledge and Kegan Paul, 1981.
Maritain, Jacques. *Man and the State.* Chicago: University of Chicago Press, 1957.
Marx, Karl and Frederick Engels. "The Holy Family, or Critique of Critical Criticism: Against Bruno Bauer and Company." In *Collected Works, vol. 4 (1844–1845),* trans. Richard Dixon and Clemens Dutt. London: Lawrence & Wishart, 1975, 8–211.
Mauss, Marcel. *The Gift: The Form and Reason for Exchange in Archaic Societies,* trans. W. D. Halls. New York: W. W. Norton, 1990.
McClure, Kirstie. "On the Subject of Rights: Pluralism, Plurality, and Political Identity." In *Dimensions of Radical Democracy: Pluralism, Citizenship, Community,* ed. Chantal Mouffe. New York: Verso, 1992, 108–27.
McHoul, Alec. "Ordinary Heterodoxies: Towards a Theory of Cultural Objects." *UTS Review* 3 (1997): 7–22.
Mellor, Stanley A. "Pragmatism at Oxford." *Boston Evening Transcript,* November 4, 1908, 18.
Menand, Louis. *The Metaphysical Club: A Story of Ideas in America.* New York: Farrar, Straus, and Giroux, 2001.

Merriman, Charles E. *Studies in the Problem of Sovereignty Since Rousseau.* New York: Columbia University Press, 1990.
Miller, Joshua L. *Democratic Temperament: The Legacy of William James.* Lawrence: University Press of Kansas, 1997.
Mills, C. Wright. *The Power Elite.* Oxford, UK: Oxford University Press, 1956.
Moore, F. C. T. *Bergson: Thinking Backwards.* Cambridge, UK: Cambridge University Press, 1996.
Mullarkey, John, ed. *The New Bergson.* Manchester, UK: Manchester University Press, 1999.
Murphy, Alexander B. "The Sovereign State System as Political-Territorial Ideal: Historical and Contemporary Considerations." In *State Sovereignty as Social Construct*, ed. Thomas J. Biersteker and Cynthia Weber. Cambridge, UK: Cambridge University Press, 1996, 81–120.
Nancy, Jean-Luc. *The Birth To Presence,* trans. Brian Holmes. Stanford, CA: Stanford University Press, 1993.
———. *The Experience of Freedom,* trans. Bridget McDonald. Stanford, CA: Stanford University Press, 1993.
Oakeshott, Michael. *On Human Conduct.* Oxford, UK: Oxford University Press, 1975.
Obatnin, Gennady. "James and Viacheslav Ivanov at the 'Threshold of Consciousness.'" In *William James and Russian Culture,* ed. Joan Delany Grossman and Ruth Rischin. Lanham, MD: Lexington, 2003, 113–29.
Perry, Ralph Barton. *In the Spirit of William James.* Bloomington: Indiana University Press, 1958.
Pitkin, Walter Boughton. "James and Bergson: Or, Who Is against Intellect?" *Journal of Philosophy, Psychology, and Scientific Method* 7 (1910): 225–31.
Poole, Randall A. "William James in the Moscow Psychological Society: Pragmatism, Pluralism, Personalism." In *William James and Russian Culture,* ed. Joan Delany Grossman and Ruth Rischin. Lanham: Lexington, 2003, 131–58
Rawls, John. *A Theory of Justice.* Cambridge, MA: Harvard University Press, 1971.
Reilly, Eliza Jane. "Concrete Possibilities: William James and the European Avant-Garde." *Streams of William James* 2 (2000): 22–29.
Riley, Jonathan. "Interpreting Berlin's Liberalism." *American Political Science Review* 95 (2001): 283–95.
Rosenau, James N. *The Study of Global Interdependence: Essays on the Transnationalism of World Affairs.* New York: Nichols, 1980.
Sallis, John. *Chorology: On Beginning in Plato's Timaeus.* Bloomington: Indiana University Press, 1999.
Sandel, Michael. *Liberalism and the Limits of Justice.* Cambridge, UK: Cambridge University Press, 1992.
Santayana, George. *Character and Opinion in the United States, with Reminiscences of William James and Josiah Royce and Academic Life in America.* New York: C. Scribner's Sons, 1920.
Scarry, Elaine. *The Body in Pain: The Making and Unmaking of the World.* Oxford, UK: Oxford University Press, 1985.
Scott's Charles E. *The Lives of Things.* Bloomington: Indiana University Press, 2002.

Scott, Joan W. "Experience." In *Feminists Theorize the Political*, ed. Judith Butler and Joan W. Scott, 22–40. New York: Routledge, 1992.

Scharfstein, Ben-Ami. *Roots of Bergson's Philosophy*. New York: Columbia University Press, 1943.

Shapiro, Michael J. *Violent Cartographies: Mapping Cultures of War*. Minneapolis: University of Minnesota Press, 1997.

Smith, Brian Cantwell. *On the Origin of Objects*. Cambridge, MA: MIT Press, 1996.

Smith, T. Vernor. *The Promise of American Politics*. Chicago: University of Chicago Press, 1936.

Sokal, Alan, and Jean Bricmont. *Fashionable Nonsense: Postmodern Intellectuals and the Abuse of Science*. New York: Picador, 1999.

Strauss, Leo. *The Rebirth of Classical Political Rationalism: An Introduction to the Thought of Leo Strauss*, ed. Thomas Pangle. Chicago: Chicago University Press, 1989.

Tavuzzi, Michael. "A Note on Husserl's Dependence on William James." *Journal of the British Society for Phenomenology* 10 (1979): 194–96.

Teuber, Marianne L. "Gertrude Stein, William James, and Pablo Picasso's Cubism." In *A Pictorial History of Psychology*, ed. Wolfgang G. Bringmann, Helmut E. Luck, Rudolf Miller, and Charles E. Early. Chicago: Quintessence Publishing, 1997, 256–64.

Todorov, Tzvetan. *The Conquest of America: The Question of the Other*, trans. Richard Howard. New York: HarperCollins, 1984.

Townsend, Kim. *Manhood at Harvard: William James and Others*. New York: W. W. Norton, 1996.

Truman, David B. *The Governmental Process: Political Interests and Public Opinion*. New York: Alfred A. Knopf, 1951.

Vasquez, John A. *The Power of Power Politics: A Critique*. New Brunswick, NJ: Rutgers University Press, 1983.

Wade, Robert. "Globalization and Its Limits: Reports of the Death of the International Economy Are Grossly Exaggerated." In *National Diversity and Global Capitalism*, ed. Suzanne Berger and Ronald Dore.Ithaca, NY: Cornell University Press, 1996, 60–88.

Wahl, Jean. *The Pluralist Philosophies of England & America*, trans. Fred Rothwell. London: Open Court Co., 1925.

Walker, R. B. J. "Forward" to *Sovereignty and Subjectivity*, ed. Jenny Edkins, Nalani Persram, and Véronique Pin-Fat. Boulder, CO: Lynne Rienner, 1999, ix–xii.

———. *One World, Many Worlds: Struggles for a Just World Peace*. Boulder, CO: Lynne Reiner, 1988.

Walzer, Michael. "The Civil Society Argument." In *Dimensions of Radical Democracy: Pluralism, Citizenship, and Democracy*, ed. Chantal Mouffe. London: Verso, 1992, 89–107.

Warner, Daniel. "Searching for Responsibility/Community in International Relations." In *Moral Spaces: Rethinking Ethics and World Politics*, ed. David Campbell and Michael Shapiro. Minneapolis: University of Minnesota Press, 1999, 1–28.

Weber, Cynthia. *Simulating Sovereignty: Intervention, the State, and Symbolic Exchange*. Cambridge, MA: Cambridge University Press, 1995.

Wendt, Alexander, and Daniel Friedheim. "Hierarchy Under Anarchy: Informal Empire and the East German State." In *State Sovereignty as Social Construct*, ed. Thomas J. Biersteker and Cynthia Weber. Cambridge, MA: Cambridge University Press, 1996, 240–77.

Williams, William Appleman. *The Tragedy of American Diplomacy*. New York, Dell: 1962.

Wolin, Sheldon. *Politics and Vision: Continuity and Innovation in Western Political Thought*. Boston: Little, Brown, 1960.

Worms, Frédéric. "James et Bergson: Lectures Croisées." *Philosophie* 64 (1999): 54–68.

Zakaras, Alex. "Isaiah Berlin's Cosmopolitan Ethics." *Political Theory* 32 (2003): 495–518.

# Index

Abbott, Lyman, 73–74
absolutism, xxii–xxiii, 7, 68; Hegelian, 53; state-centered, 19, 34; systemic, 33
academics, American, 51
Adorno, Theodor, 51
Agamben, Giorgio, 78
agonistics, 24, 27
agoraphilia, 90
agoraphobia, 89–91
anarchism, 19
Anglo-American philosophy. *See* Anglo-American theory
Anglo-American theory, xxiv, 52–53, 65
anti-foundationalism, 51, 63
anti-Hegelian, 15, 17, 58
anti-imperialism, xxi, xxiv, 34, 42–44
anti-materialism, 81
anti-rationalism, 67
anti-Semitism, 62
anti-Soviet, 64
anti-teleology, 54
anti-vivisection, xxi
Appadurai, Arjun, 12n14
appearance, 80
Arendt, Hannah, 24, 27, 86n38
art, 78

artifacts, 78
Ashley, Richard, 39
associations, 17
Atkinson, Edward, 43
authority, theological, 35
Ayer, A. J., 9

baby, 75
Bacon, Francis, 79
Bayle, Pierre, 75
being, multiplicity of, 54
Bentley, Arthur, 16
Berlin, Isaiah, 9, 14n31, 16, 24–25; value incommensurability of, 24
Bergson, Henri, xxiv, 52–68, 76, 83, 92
Berkeley, Bishop George, 4
Bodin, Jean, 34–36
Bohman, James, 31n47
Boodin, John, 73–74

"cabinets of wonder." *See wunderkammern*
Calvino, Italo, 84
Campbell, David, 35, 39
capital: international, 39; transnational, 34

capitalism, 90; global, 39
Certeau, Michel de, 13n28, 92
children, 24
China, 38
Christianity, 61
citizens, 22, 37
citizenship, 35
City of God, 81
civil liberty, 46
Civil Rights Movement, 24, 90
class conflict, 75
Cold War, 34, 39
Cole, G. D. H., xxiv, 17–22, 28
colonialism, 39, 43
Commons, 18
communism, 25, 67, 75
computers, 82–83
Connolly, William, 13n28
consciousness, 60, 76–77
constitutions, pluralist, 27
Continental philosophy. *See* Continental theory
Continental theory, xxiv, 52–53, 64, 66–67
corporations, 17
*Creative Evolution*, 54, 58, 63
criminals, 10
Cubans, 46
cubism, 62
cybernetics, 82

Dahl, Robert A., xxiv, 16, 22–24, 40
Darwin, Charles, 54
Deleuze, Gilles, 51, 55, 62–63, 68; and Félix Guattari, 13n27
democracy, xxiii, 21–22, 27, 90–91
Der Derian, James, 39
Derrida, Jacques, 51
Descartes, René, 75, 79–80, 86n28
Deutsche, Rosalyn, 89
Dewey, John, xxii, 2, 5, 14n37, 16, 28n2
difference, 5, 8–11, 15, 16, 19–21, 27, 40–41
discourse, political, 6
dissent, 27, 42, 46–47
dogs, 11

Doty, Roxanne Lynn, 45
Douglass, Frederick, 90–91
dualism, theoretical, 55
DuBois, W. E. B., 91
Duguit, Léon, 38
Duns Scotus, John, 75
duration, 54–55, 58
Durkheim, Émile, 67

earthquake, 61
economism, 27
Eisenberg, Avigail, 14n37
empiricism, 2, 4, 52; American radical, 66–67, 81; multiplicity of, 55
Emerson, Ralph Waldo, 68n2
Engels, Friedrich, 75
Enloe, Cynthia, 39
epistemology, Bergson's, 59
Europe, xxiv, 36–37, 51–53, 64–65, 67, 77; medieval, 77–78
European history, 77
evolution, 54
exceptionalism, American, 90
existentialism, 62, 66–67

facism, xxii, 25
faith, religious, 2, 8
Faulkner, William, 56
fauvism, 62
Fechner, Gustav, 16, 58
federalism, 18, 20
federalist, radical, 18
feminism, 24
feudalism, economic, 35
fictions, 38
field, 60
Figgis, J. N., xxiv, 17–20, 22, 28
Filipinos, xxiv, 43–46
*Finnegans Wake*, 62
Flathman, Richard, 12n15
Florentine Pragmatic Club, 65
Flournoy, Théodore, 7, 66
formalism, 24
Foucault, Michel, 51, 68, 86n28; historiography of, 90

France, 62, 65, 67; Vichy, 67
free speech, 90
freedom, 4, 22, 27, 36; negative, 26–27
Freud, Sigmund, 7, 57
futurism, 62

gay: activists, 90; and lesbian rights, 6, 24
*Geist*, 34
genealogy, intellectual, 68
general will, 21, 33
globalization, 42; opposition to, 46
God, 61, 77–79, 87n39
Godkin, E. L., 43
government: democratic, 46; U.S., 22
Gray, John, 14n31
Guattari, Felix, 63
guilds, 19

Hardt, Michael, 39
harmony, 54
Harvard, 52
Hawai'i, 34: monarchy of, 42
Hawaiians, 46
Hegel, G. F., xxii–xxiii, 2, 4, 17, 19, 23, 25, 33, 36, 42, 46, 52–53, 58, 80, 84, 92
Heidegger, Martin, 51, 62, 80
hermeneutics, 45
heroism, Emersonian, 1
heterodoxy, 92
heterosexuality, 6
hippies, 89
Hinsley, F. H., 37
history, 90; great consensus of, 89; pluralist reading of, 91
Hobbes, Thomas, 33–36, 75; state of nature, 35
Holmes, Oliver Wendell, 18
*The Holy Family*, 75
Holy Roman Empire, 37
homogenization, global
homosexuality, 6
Hsiao, Kung Chuan, xxiv, 15, 20–21, 30n29
Hulme, T. E., 64

human nature, 25
human rights, 11, 46; organizations, 38
Hume, David, 16, 75
Huntington, Samuel, 22
hyphenism, 20

idealism, 40
idealist, 81
identities: national, 44; political, 23
individualism, 33, 35, 54
influences, Jamesian, 52
imagination, 52, 57, 80
immigrants, Mexican, 90
imperialism, 7, 33, 42–43, 65, 90; American, 43; McKinleyite, 42; United States's, 34, 42; Western, 39
Indians, American, 44
intellectual history, xxiii, 52–53, 63, 68, 79
intellectualism, 55, 58, 60
international relations, 34, 40; realism, 37; scholars of, 38
internationalization, 42
interstate relations, 38
interventionism, American, 44
intuition, 55, 58, 69n8
isolationism, 4, 43

Jew, 67
Jim Crow, 7
Jones, Matthew L., 86n32
Joyce, James, 62
judgment, 74

Kallen, Horace, 65–66
Kant, Immanuel, xxii, xxiv, 2, 11, 80, 92
Kariel, Henry, 23–24
Kaufman-Osborn, Timothy, 28n2
Keenan, Thomas, 89
King, Jr., Martin Luther, 91
Krasner, Steven, 39

Lake Chautauqua, 1, 7, 27; The Assembly at, 1–2
language, 55–56

Laski, Harold, xxiv, 15, 17–22, 25, 28, 38
Latour, Bruno, 12n13, 51
legitimacy, 27, 41
Leibnitz, Gottfried, 60, 92
Lenin, V. I., 64
Lefort, Claude, 89
LeRoy, Henry, 75
Leviathan, 35
Levinas, Emmanuel, 57
liberalism, 9–11, 14n31, 40–41; anti-political, 27; Wilsonian, 46
liberty, 18, 26, 34, 44
Lilydale, 1–2
Lingis, Alphonso, 82
Locke, John, 75, 92
Lukács, Georg, 62
Lutoslawski, Wincenty, 16
Lyotard, François, 51
Lynching, 7, 90

MacIver, R. M., 38
Mackenzie, W. J., 24
Magid, Henry Meyer, 21–22, 30n34
Maitland, Frederic, 16
majoritarianism, democratic, 23, 47
Maritain, Jacques, 38
Marx, Karl, xxii, 75–76, 80, 84
Marxism, 51, 76
materialism, 75–76, 84; heterodox, 92
Mauss, Marcel, 73
McHoul, Alec, 84
McKinley, William, 42–43
*mémoire.* See memory
memory, 54, 56–58
Menand, Louis, 66, 71n71
Ménard, Louis, 16
Merleau-Ponty, Maurice, 51, 62
Merriman, Charles, 38
metaphysics, 56, 59–60, 62, 68, 75
Mexico, 22
militarism, 8
Mill, John Stuart, 26
Mills, C. Wright, 24
minority, 23; rights, 46
modernism, 64

modernity, 3–4, 7; birth of, 77; high, 77
monadism, 2–3, 23
monism, 7, 25, 66
"The Moral Equivalent of War," 7
Moscow Psychological Society, 64
Mugwumpery, 43
multiculturalism, 28
multiplicity. *See* pluralism
multiverse, xxiii, 54, 60
Murphy, Timothy, 55
mysticism, 61; anti-positivist, 64

Nancy, Jean-Luc, 13n28, 77
nanotechnology, 82
*The Nation,* 43
nation-states, 36, 39–40
national autonomy, 34
nationalism, 45; economic, 25
nationhood, 33
nature, 41, 78
natural science, 75
nativism, 44
Negri, Antonio, 39
networks, 8
*The New York Evening Post,* 43
Nietzsche, Friedrich, xxii, 62, 64, 68n2
nostalgia, 90

Oakeshott, Michael, 9
object-oriented system design, xxv, 82
*On the Origin of Objects,* 82
"the one and the many," 3
oneness, 33
onticology, 82
orthodoxy, 92
Oxford, 58

pacifism, xxi, 7, 42
Pascal, Blaise, 79
past, 56
Peace of Westphalia, 36
perceptions, xxiv, 79–80
Picasso, Pablo, 64
Pierce, C. S., 2, 5, 60, 68n2
Pitkin, Walter, 66

## Index

phenomenology, 62
Philippines, 34, 42–45
planes, 56–57
Plato, 81, 86n38, 92
Platonists, 51
pluralism, xxi, xxv, 2, 5–8, 14n31, 15, 19–20, 21–27, 40, 42, 54–56, 59–60, 63–64, 66, 68, 74, 83, 85, 90–91; absolute, 3; abstract, 22; American, 66–67; American cultural, 20; anti-Hegelian, 16; Bergsonian, 58, 63; Berlinian, 9, 26; concrete, 22; critics of formalism, 24; decline of, 27; Deleuzian, 63; empirical, 61; English political, 25; formalist, 16, 22–24, 26–28; individual, 43; institutional, 6, 10, 16, 22; international, 46; Jamesian, xxiii–xxiv, 4–5, 9–11, 19, 21, 23, 26–28, 33, 40, 42, 45–47, 52–54, 58, 64, 68, 74, 83–84, 91; latter-day, 26–27, 40; legal, 21; liberal, 9–10, 27–28; political, 28, 40, 92; self-congratulatory, 28; theories of, 16–17; universalist, 15
pluralist school, the, 18
pluralistic outlook, 83, 92
*A Pluralistic Universe*, 2, 18, 53, 58, 60
pluriverse, xxiii
politics, xxii, 91–92
political theory, xxii, 8, 16–17, 22–24, 27, 33, 91; American, 16; depoliticization of, 27; traditional, 33
political science, xxii, 26
positivism, 67, 75
post-imperialist, 46
postmodernism, 51, 68
poststructuralism, 51
*Pragmatism*, 53, 59, 75
*Principles of Psychology*, 3
"pragmaticism," 2
pragmatism, xxi, xxv, 5, 16, 20, 42, 52, 59, 60, 64–67, 73–74, 81–82, 84, 91; American, 66–67
predetermination, 57
*Principles of Psychology*, 59, 61

Proudhon, Pierre-Joseph, 16
Proust, Marcel, 62
psychology, xxi, xxiii, 7, 42, 52, 65, 67, 91

"radical empiricist," 67
racial equality, 24
racism, xxi
rationalism, 67
Rawls, John, 9–10, 14n33
"realism," 37
reality, 77
"Reflections on Little Rock," 24
Reilly, Eliza Jane, 64–65
relativism, 4
religion, 60
rattle, 75
*Remembrance of Things Past*, 62
Renouvier, Charles Bernard, 16
representation, 24, 27
*Revue Philosophique*, 67
rhizome, 63
rights, 46
robber barons, 89
Roosevelt, Theodore, 42
Rorty, Richard, xxii
Rousseau, Jean-Jacques, 21, 33, 36
Russia, 64
Russian thought, 65

Sandel, Michael, 14n33
Santayana, George, 9
Scarry, Elaine, 75
science, 56, 64
self, xxii–xxiii, 56–57, 59, 75–76, 90
self-determination, 46; Wilsonian, 40
self-governance, 42
sensation, 74–76
senses, 79; human, 74
sexualities, 6
Shapiro, Michal, 39
Simmel, Georg, 62
skepticism, 4
slaves, 10
Smith, Brian Cantwell, 82–83
Smith, T. Vernor, 30n36

socialism, 75; guild, 19
Socrates, 84
solipsism, 4, 77
Sophists, 51
souls, 44
sovereignty, xxii, 19–20, 27, 33–39, 42–43, 45–47; constituted nature of, 38; fascist, 40; Hobbesian, 37; inconsistencies of, 35; international, 37; interstate, 36; Jamesian, 39–40; language of, 38; pluralist conceptions of, 34; pro-American, 46; state, 37; Wilsonian, 40
Soviet, 64
space, 81
Spain, 42, 65
Spanish-American War, 42
Spencer, Herbert, 87n39
Spinoza, Baruch, 92
spiritualist, 81
Stanford University, 61
state, xxii, 17–23, 33, 35–38; pluralistic theory of, 17; rights of, 40
state power, 22, 35–36
statecraft, xxii
statism, 22
Stein, Gertrude, 64
streams, 76
*Studies in the Problem of Sovereignty*, 17
suffrage, universal, 46
supernaturalism, 60
Symbolists, Russian, 64

Taft, William Howard, 44
technologies, information and communication, 34
terrorism, 34
Teuber, Marianne, 64
"thing-in-itself," 80–81
things, 3, 74–77, 79–84, 92
*A Thousand Plateaus*, 63
time, xxv, 54–56, 58, 62, 81
*Time and Free Will*, 67
toleration, 26

totalitarianism, xxii
transcendentalism, 66
Treaty of Westphalia, 36–37
*trompe l'oeil*, 78
Truman, David, xxiv, 22–24, 30n29
truth, 8, 51, 58, 62, 64, 74, 77, 81; epistemological, 79; universality of, 91
truth claims, 51
Truth, Sojourner, 91
*The Two Sources of Morality and Religion*, 61

*Under the Banner of Socialism*, 65
United States, xxiv, 7, 9, 20, 24, 34, 38, 42–46, 52, 65, 67, 89, 90–91
universalism, 7–8, 10, 15, 18, 28, 77, 91
universe, xxiii, 59–60
U.S.S. *Maine*, 42
utopia, 1–2, 7, 27

*The Varieties of Religious Experience*, 64
venison, 76
Virgil, 74
virtual, 57

Walker, R. B. J., 36, 39
Walzer, Michael, 10
war, xxiii
Warner, Daniel, 36
wax, 79
Weber, Cynthia, 39
Wells, Ida B., 91
West, Cornell, xxii
wife, 73
wilderness, 41
Wilson, Woodrow, 40
women, 10
Worms, Frédéric, 57
*wunderkammern*, 78

Young, Iris Marion, 89

Zeno's arrow, 55

# About the Author

**Kennan Ferguson** teaches political theory and international relations at the University of South Florida, where he is director of interdisciplinary social sciences. He is the author of *The Politics of Judgment: Aesthetics, Identity, and Political Theory* (1999).